Atkins Diet Air Fryer Cookbook

Low Carb Atkins Diet Air Fryer Recipes to To Lose Weight Rapidly, Stay Healthy and Be Longevity

By Bove Hughes

© Copyright 2019 -Bove Hughes -All rights reserved.

In no way is it legal to reproduce, duplicate, or transmit any part of this document by either electronic means or in printed format. Recording of this publication is strictly prohibited, and any storage of this material is not allowed unless with written permission from the publisher. All rights reserved.

The information provided herein is stated to be truthful and consistent, in that any liability, regarding inattention or otherwise, by any usage or abuse of any policies, processes, or directions contained within is the solitary and complete responsibility of the recipient reader. Under no circumstances will any legal liability or blame be held against the publisher for any reparation, damages, or monetary loss due to the information herein, either directly or indirectly. Respective authors own all copyrights not held by the publisher.

Legal Notice:

This book is copyright protected. This is only for personal use. You cannot amend, distribute, sell, use, quote or paraphrase any part or the content within this book without the consent of the author or copyright owner. Legal action will be pursued if this is breached.

Disclaimer Notice:

Please note the information contained within this document is for educational and entertainment purposes only. Every attempt has been made to provide accurate, up to date and reliable, complete information. No warranties of any kind are expressed or implied. Readers acknowledge that the author is not engaging in the rendering of legal, financial, medical or professional advice.

By reading this document, the reader agrees that under no circumstances are we responsible for any losses, direct or indirect, which are incurred as a result of the use of information contained within this document, including, but not limited to, —errors, omissions, or inaccuracies.

Table of Contents

Introduction 7
Chapter 1 Essentials of Atkins Diet 9
What is the Atkins diet? 9
The History of Atkins Diet 9
How Does It Work? 9
Why it is Effective for Weight Loss? 10
The Benefits of the Atkins Diet 11
Atkins Diet Step-by-Step 11
    Phase 1: Induction 11
    Phase 2: Balancing 12
    Phase 3: Fine Tuning 13
    Phase 4: Maintenance 14
What Groceries Will I Need to Get Started? 15
What Can I Eat? 17
    Phase 1: 17
    Phase 2. 21
    Phase 3. 22
    Phase 4. 23
What Should I Avoid? 24
Chapter 2: Everything About the Air Fryer 26
    What is An Air Fryer? 26
    The Benefits of The Air Fryers 27
    Air Fryer vs. Traditional Fryer 27
    The Various Air Fryer Brands 29
    Phillips XL Air fryer 29
    GoWISE USA GW22621 Electric Air Fryer 30
    Power Air Fryer XL 30
    Avalon Bay Digital Air Fryer 31
    NuWave Brio Air Fryer 31

How to Use an Air Fryer...31
Preparation...32
Pre-Heating..32
Cooking..32
Cleaning...32
How to Clean & Maintain An Air Fryer...32
How to clean your air fryer..32
How to maintain your air fryer..33
How to Choose a Good Air Fryer..33
What affects the buyer's decision of your air fryer?...33
Tips on how to choose the air fryer best for you...34
Where to Buy a Good Air Fryer?...35
Air Frying Compatible Foods..35
Frozen Foods..35
Raw Meat...35
Vegetables..35
Baked Goods..35
Roasting Nuts...35
Wet-Battered Foods...36
FAQs of Air Fryer..36
1. Can we cook various kinds of food in the air fryer?..36
2. How long does it take to cook frozen foods?...36
3. How much can I cook in my air fryer?...36
4. Is there any specific kind of oils needed for air frying?..36
5. Can I add more ingredients while the food is getting cooked in my air fryer?.......36
6. Can I use a baking paper or aluminum foil in my air fryer?...................................36
7. Is preheating required before I cook?..37

Chapter 3: Air Fryer Breakfast Recipes..38
Delicious Breakfast Souffle...38
Yummy Breakfast Italian Frittata..39
Savory Cheese and Bacon Muffins...40

Best Air-Fried English Breakfast..41

Chapter 4: Air Fryer Lunch Recipes...42

Incredible Air-Fried Burgers...42

Extraordinary Stuffed Zucchini with Bacon and Jalapeno............................43

Good-Tasting Turkey Rolls..44

Chapter 5: Air Fryer Dinner Recipes..45

General Wong's Beef and Broccoli..45

Irresistible Meatloaf...46

Rockstar Rib Eye-Steak...47

Super-Yummy Roast Pork Belly..48

Outstanding Rack of Lamb..49

Phenomenal Herbed Roast Beef...50

Amazing Lamb Chops with Herbed Garlic Sauce.......................................51

Chapter 6: Air Fryer Appetizer Recipes...52

Astonishing Chicken Kebabs..52

Appetizing Avocado Fries...53

Godly Pork Taquitos..54

Gratifying Stuffed Mushrooms..55

Everyday Chicken Nuggets...56

Chapter 7: Air Fryer Poultry Recipes...57

Flavorful Fried Chicken...57

Delectable Whole Roast Chicken..58

Divine Buffalo Wings...59

Flavorsome Honey Lime Chicken Wings..60

Delightful Coconut Crusted Chicken Tenders...61

Well-Tasted Popcorn Chicken...62

Easy Chicken Strips..63

Savory Sriracha Chicken Drumsticks..64

Chinese-Style Honey Garlic Chicken..65

Rich Parmesan Crusted Chicken Breasts...66

Nashville Flaming Hot Breaded Chicken...67

Desirable Korean Fried Chicken Wings..69

Awesome Crispy Baked Garlic Parmesan Chicken Wings..70

Spicy Teriyaki Chicken Wings..71

Chapter 8: Air Fryer Fish and Seafood..72

Remarkable Fish and Chips with Sauce..72

Grand Air-Fried Coconut Shrimp..74

Splendid Salmon Patties..75

Japanese-Style Fried Prawns...76

Great Air-Fried Soft-Shell Crab..77

Stunning Air-Fried Clams..78

Mind-Blowing Air-Fried Crawfish with Cajun Dipping Sauce..79

Southern-Air-Fried Cat Fish..80

Wondrous Creole Fried Shrimp with Sriracha Sauce...81

Chapter 9: Air Fryer Meat Recipes..82

Sweet and Spicy Montreal Steak...82

Stunning Chicken Sandwich..83

Hearty Hot Dogs..84

Sweet and Sour Pork..85

Yummy Rodeo Sirloin Steaks with Coffee Rub..86

Chapter 10: Air Fryer Vegetable and Sides Recipes..87

Supreme Air-Fried Tofu..87

Not Your Average Zucchini Parmesan Chips...88

Outstanding Batter-Fried Scallions...89

Delectable French Green Beans with Shallots and Almonds...90

Super-Healthy Air-Fried Green Tomatoes..91

Luscious Air-Fried Broccoli Crisps...92

Chapter 11: Air Fryer Desert Recipes..93

Toothsome Caramel Cheesecake...93

Conclusion..95

Introduction

Hi friend! This is Bove Hughes. Firstly, I'd like to thank and congratulate you for reading this book: "***Atkins Diet Air Fryer Cookbook- Low Carb Atkins Diet Air Fryer Recipes to To Lose Weight Rapidly, Stay Healthy and Be Longevity***". I hope this book will bring you the support and guidance you're looking for!

Are you tired from all of your failed weight loss attempts? Do you want to enjoy fried foods and still maintain yet a healthier version of your body? **Are you tired of wasting time and oil in the kitchen?** Are you searching for an easy-to-use kitchen gadget that can bake, grill, and fry in a matter of minutes? If you answered yes to any of the above, then you are certainly at the right spot. Keep reading! You will find all the answers!

The Atkins diet is ideal for people who are struggling to lose weight. This cookbook will guide you through your journey towards a healthy body and help you achieve your goals. It will help you understand what exactly the Atkins diet is, and how it works to benefit your body.

There are four phases you will go through while following the Atkins diet. With this cookbook, you will learn about each phase and its respective diet plan. Along with this information, this cookbook will also help you understand the changes you'll be making in your lifestyle, and will guide you through the little tips and tricks that make a difference.

The Atkins Diet involves and encourages a lot of Air Fryer cooking. Wondering why exactly you should cook your meals with Air Fryer? Don't fret; this cookbook will explain all of the benefits that make Air Fryer cooking such an essential part of the Atkins diet. There are over 50 easy-to-follow Air Fryer recipes. A variety of recipes are included, covering **beef, pork, chicken, turkey, vegetable, fish and seafood, vegetables, appetizers and dessert, etc.**.

The Atkins Diet might seem like a long and tough journey, but with proper guidance and support, you'll find what you've been looking for and fulfill your desired goals.

This book contains proven steps and strategies on how to use your Air Fryer to make Atkins Diet recipes, faster than ever. These easy Air Fryer recipes are simple to make, taste delicious and give a multitude of nutrients to keep you happy and healthy. According to common belief, using the Air Fryer requires an advanced set of cooking skills, but that's completely untrue! This book will teach you how to use it to prepare food faster. With your Air Fryer, you'll be eating healthy Atkins Diet foods every day without spending too much time in the kitchen. So, let's get started!

Chapter 1 Essentials of Atkins Diet

What is the Atkins diet?
Simply put, the Atkins diet is a low-carb, high-protein and high-fat diet. It's designed to help people struggling to lose weight and achieve their body goals. Followed properly, the Atkins diet is part of a healthy lifestyle.

The History of Atkins Diet
The Atkins Diet was developed in the early 1970's by a cardiologist named Robert C. Atkins, and it quickly gained a large following. Diets were common in the early 20th century, but all of the popular diets were temporary "quick fixes" based on deprivation or bizarre food choices. They focused on net calories per meal, instead of on the holistic notion of a permanent change to one's way of eating. Dr. Atkins was one of the first proponents of the idea that weight loss could be part of a healthy, sustainable lifestyle. The Atkins Diet is also backed by multiple scientific studies.

How Does It Work?
People's bodies respond differently to different stimuli; some people require a higher protein intake, while others do better when limiting carb intake. What the Atkins Diet does is allow each person to determine what type of food suits them and their metabolism.

There are two types of energy sources the body can use: sugar and fats. It's important to understand that the particular type of fuel you burn will affect how you lose weight and whether you can maintain the weight loss or not. Regular diets are focused solely on reducing calorie intake, but they don't account for the amount or proportion of fats, protein and carbohydrates that you consume.

Many years' worth of research has shown that the Atkins Diet is a safe and effective way to lose body fat and then maintain your desired weight level for as long as the plan is followed, which is not hard to do if you approach the diet knowing that it represents long-term change for you and your body.

Why it is Effective for Weight Loss?

When you eat, your body turns the carbohydrates in your food into sugar, specifically glucose, during digestion. Your metabolism runs on glucose, so your body likes to keep a 24-hour supply on hand, in the form of glycogen. Glycogen is your body's fuel source of choice. If you don't use your entire supply of glycogen within 24 hours, the unused glycogen will be deposited within your body as fat, and a new glycogen supply will be drawn from the food you consume. It's a constant cycle.

Unless your glycogen supply is exhausted, your body will not burn fat. Fat is your body's long-term energy storage solution; it's what keeps you alive when there's no food available, like during a famine. Your body has evolved to maintain fat storage for the sake of survival.

What all this means is that a high carbohydrate intake will keep your glycogen stores constantly full, which will prevent your body from burning fat, despite your best efforts with diet and exercise. The Atkins Diet helps you solve this problem in the following ways:

1. By reducing your daily carbohydrate intake, you will run through your glycogen stores more quickly and cause your body to burn more fat for energy. This not only helps in reducing the overall fat content of the body, but also ensures that the limited amount of carbohydrates taken in by the body are not left unused and converted to fat.

2. Since your calorie intake remains roughly the same, you shouldn't struggle with hunger or feeling deprived. Your body gets a stable source of energy- but just enough energy instead of too much. You should still feel energetic and satisfied, while you continue to lose weight. You may even find that foods recommended for the Atkins Diet are not that different from foods in your regular diet before.

3. You can customize the Atkins Diet for your specific needs, and that flexibility is what makes the Atkins Diet so sustainable for long-term change.

The Benefits of the Atkins Diet
The Atkins Diet delivers a considerable number of benefits, including:

1. Promoting effective weight loss;
2. Providing an understanding of your bodily needs;
3. Helping to decide which foods are best for your body;
4. Helping to maintain energy levels throughout the day;
5. Helping to avoid hunger-related temptations;
6. Allowing you to sustain a long-term healthy lifestyle .

Atkins Diet Step-by-Step
The Atkins Diet is a low-carb diet and is often recommended for those who want to lose weight, while still eating the same amount of protein and fats as before, but reducing carb intake. Low-carb diets have proven to be effective at reducing weight and the Atkins Diet is one of the most reputable forms of the low-carb diet. Here is a description of the Atkins 20 Diet:

Phase 1: Induction
The purpose of the induction phase is to introduce your body to fat-burning mode. The goal is to drop your daily carb intake the current level all the way down to an average of 20 grams (18 grams minimum, and 22 maximum) daily. This will lead to a smaller daily glycogen supply, which will allow the body to start burning fats earlier in the day once the glycogen is used up. This phase will last at least two weeks, though if you wish to burn more fat, you may continue for longer periods of time without a problem. Either way, you'll continue this phase until you are 15 pounds away from your goal. Here are some tips for eating in the induction phase:

- Eat three meals and two snacks a day, or even six small meals a day. The goal is to avoid becoming so hungry that you eat whatever is on hand; you want to eat each meal intentionally. Don't go more than three or four waking hours without eating.
- Consume 20 grams of Net Carbohydrates (NC) a day. Make sure most of these come from vegetables; about 12 – 15 grams.

- Make sure to include protein with every meal. You need protein to develop muscle mass, which will help with weight loss because muscle mass burns calories even at rest. In Phase 1, the recommendation is to consume three 4 – 6-ounce servings each day.
- Don't restrict your fat intake. Fats are important for many reasons; they help to make you feel full after eating a meal, contribute to the flavor of foods, and help your body absorb certain vitamins. Fat intake is crucial to the Atkins Diet.
- Drink at least eight 8-ounce servings of water throughout the day. This accounts for your entire fluid intake, so two of your "water" servings can be coffee or tea, and another two can be beef, chicken, or vegetable broth.
- You will initially experience some water loss; this is normal, but make sure to avoid dehydration or electrolyte imbalance. Helpful sources of sodium include salty broth, table salt, and soy sauce.
- Use sugar substitutes in moderation; three packets a day at most.
- Use only Atkins products where possible, since they have been tested to ensure minimal impact on your blood sugar level. Almost all Atkins products are suitable for Phase 1. Make sure that the remaining 5 – 8 grams of your daily carbohydrates come from either Atkins products, dairy or dressings (the rest being from vegetables).

You can enjoy some slow-cooked Italian beef or poached salmon during this phase.

Phase 2: Balancing

The purpose of this phase is to start transitioning from weight loss to maintenance, by find a balance of carbohydrates in your diet. Start at 25 grams daily, and raise your intake in 5-gram steps. Depending on a variety of factors, including but not limited to age, gender, activity level and/or hormonal status, your carb level can balance out at 30 – 80 grams a day. This phase continues until you are 10 pounds away from your goal weight. However, you can move to Phase 3 earlier; your weight loss will continue but at a slower rate compared to Phase 2. Here are some tips for eating in Phase 2:

- Continue to consume a minimum of 12–15 daily grams of Net Carbohydrates as vegetables. This Phase 1 rule is continued into Phase 2. Vegetables are rich

in fiber and have the type of carbohydrates your body really needs. They are crucial to the Atkins diet.
- Follow a "carb ladder" and reintroduce foods to your diet one at a time. The intervals of adding foods may vary depending on your metabolism and weight-loss goal. You might follow weekly intervals, biweekly intervals or even longer.
- Add carbs back to your diet with each step of the ladder, one by one. For example, when you reintroduce one carb-heavy food, gauge the impact, if any, before reintroducing another one.
- Increase your overall daily Net Carb intake. Use no more than 5-gram increments on a weekly, bi-weekly or monthly interval.
- You will likely experience plateaus: times when you don't see much progress with regards to weight loss. If this happens, first double-check that you're doing everything correctly. If you are, and still not seeing the differences you want to see, it is recommended to add a bit of exercise to your routine.

Chicken and Kale soup is one of the most delicious dishes you can enjoy during this phase.

Phase 3: Fine Tuning

The purpose of this phase is to lose the last of your excess weight and further explore your carb balance; in this phase, you will find your ideal daily carb intake to maintain your weight. This phase is often considered preparation for lifelong weight maintenance. The goal here is to steadily increase your daily net carb intake in 10-gram steps, and to continue to reintroduce new carb-heavy foods so long as your weight is maintained. This phase will last till you have reached your goal weight and then afterwards, for another month of maintaining that weight. Here are some tips for eating in the fine-tuning phase:

- If You Hit a Plateau: As in Phase 2, first double-check that you're doing everything correctly; it's easy to get complacent and start to let things slip over time. If you are following the diet correctly and still not seeing progress, decrease your daily Net Carb intake by 10 grams and monitor for signs of progress.

- Finding Net Carb Tolerance: It is possible to stumble upon your Net Carb tolerance for weight maintenance in Phase 3; if you do, it might initially look like a plateau. Decrease 10 grams of your daily Net Carbohydrates for at least a week to see if this is the case. If weight loss resumes, go up another 5 grams, and so forth.

Enjoy some braised cabbage while you're in this phase. You can go through the recipes in this book to treat yourself with dishes that perfectly follow the Atkins Diet.

Phase 4: Maintenance

The purpose of this phase is to transition to a permanent weight-maintaining lifestyle. The goal here is to control your weight in case your carb tolerance changes, or if you gain some extra weight. This phase lasts indefinitely. If you are willing to adopt Phase 4 as a new lifestyle, then you may never need to diet again, since you now understand your bodily needs and compatibility with different types of foods. You have gone through the Atkins diet phase-by-phase, and have gradually developed a sustainable, healthy way of eating. Since you added foods back one at a time, you already know their effects, if any, on your body weight (regardless of whether those effects were permanent or not). You now understand which foods are best for maintaining your weight. You should also how to handle your cravings, how to substitute certain low-carb foods for high-carb ones, and how to enjoy other foods sparingly, as garnishes or finishing touches. Here is a tip for eating in the maintenance phase:

- If you have gained a few pounds, no problem; just cut roughly 10 grams of Net Carbohydrates a day from your intake until you return to your goal weight.

Travel Tips for Atkins Dieters:

1) Check if you will have access to a refrigerator during your stay, and stock up on Atkins-approved snacks.
2) If you know the restaurants where you'll be dining, check out the menu in advance to pre-select your low-carb options. Having a plan before you go out to eat makes it easier resist any high- carb temptations.

3) Try to stick with your usual meal schedule.
4) Inquire about what is in the dishes you are served, both at home and while eating out.
5) Eat only until you feel satisfied, not stuffed.
6) Drink alcohol in moderation if you are past the first phase of Atkins, and watch out for drinks containing sugar or fruit juice.
7) If your host pressures you to try something like cake or pie, politely decline by saying you're full, or eat a very small amount.
8) Offer to bring a low-carb option when attending an event in someone else's home.
9) Stay hydrated. Keep a water bottle with you and refill it frequently.
10) Stay active. Go for walks and try joining a gym or working out regularly.

What Groceries Will I Need to Get Started?

When starting out on the Atkins diet, there are some items you will need to stock up on, especially in Phase 1. Below is a list of groceries to buy when following the Atkins diet.

Vegetables are a key part of Phase 1 of the Atkins Diet; you should be getting approximately 12 to 15 grams of Net Carbohydrates per day from vegetables. Once you hit Phase 2, you'll be allowed to incorporate certain fruits.

Salad Bases

- Romaine lettuce, Iceberg lettuce
- Arugula, Spinach, Endive

Snacks

- Celery, Cucumber, Bell Peppers

Salad Toppers

- Mushrooms, Avocadoes, Artichokes
- Radicchio, Radishes

Meat: All meat is allowed during all phases of Atkins. Here are some ideas:

- Bacon, Beef, Ham, Lamb, Pork

Poultry

- Chicken, Cornish Hen, Duck, Turkey

Seafood: All fish and shellfish are allowed in all phases of Atkins. Here are some ideas:

Fish

- Salmon, Tuna, Trout
- Cod, Halibut, Shellfish

Clams

- Crabmeat, Mussels, Oysters, Shrimp

Dairy

- Sour Cream, Mayonnaise

Cheese: The following cheeses are allowed in all phases of Atkins:

- Bleu , Cheddar , Goat , Cream Cheese
- Feta , American Cheese, Gouda
- Mozzarella, Parmesan, Swiss

Refrigerator Staples

- Eggs, Salad Dressings
- Lemon Juice, Lime Juice

Pantry Staples

- Chicken or Vegetable Broth or Bouillon Cubes, Splenda, Vegetable Oil
- Olive Oil, Herbs and Spices

Beverages

- Flavored Zero-Calorie Seltzer Water
- Diet Soda, Club Soda, Coffee, Tea

What Can I Eat?

Each of the four phases of the Atkins diet has its own food requirements. Here is a breakdown of acceptable foods at each phase of the Atkins diet:

Phase 1:

Foundation Vegetables	SERVING SIZE	NET CARBS
Alfalfa sprouts (raw)	1/2 cup	0
Chicory greens (raw)	1/2 cup	0.1
Endive (raw)	1/2 cup	0.1
Escarole (raw)	1/2 cup	0.1
Olives, green	5, each	0.1
Watercress (raw)	1/2 cup	0.1
Arugula (raw)	1/2 cup	0.2
Radishes (raw)	1, each	0.2
Spinach (raw)	1/2 cup	0.2
Bok choy (cooked)	1/2 cup	0.4
Lettuce, average (raw)	1/2 cup	0.5
Turnip greens (cooked)	1/2 cup	0.6
Heart of palm	1 each	0.7
Beet greens (cooked)	1/2 cup	1.8
Olives, black	5, each	0.7
Radicchio (raw)	1/2 cup	0.7
Asparagus (cooked)	6 stalks	1.9
Eggplant (cooked)	1/2 cup	2.3
Sprouts, mung beans (raw)	1/2 cup	2.2
Button mushrooms (raw)	1/2 cup	0.8
Artichoke (marinated)	1, each	1
Celery (raw)	1 stalk	1
Collard greens (cooked)	1/2 cup	1
Pickle, dill	1, each	1
Broccoli (cooked)	1/2 cup	1.8
Rhubarb (raw)	1/2 cup	1.8
Cucumber, sliced (raw)	1/2 cup	1.6
Spinach	1/2 cup	1
Broccoli rabe (cooked)	1/2 cup	1.2
Sauerkraut (drained)	1/2 cup	1.2
Avocado, Haas	1/2 fruit	1.3
Daikon radish, grated (raw)	1/2 cup	1.4
Red/white onion, chopped (raw)	2 TBSP	1.5
Zucchini (cooked)	1/2 cup	1.5
Cauliflower (cooked)	1/2 cup	1.7
Fennel (raw)	1/2 cup	1.8
Okra (cooked)	1/2 cup	1.8
Swiss chard (cooked)	1/2 cup	1.8
Broccoli (cooked)	3, each	1.9

	Serving Size	Net Carbs
Bell pepper, green, chopped (raw)	1/2 cup	2.2
Kale (cooked)	1/2 cup	2.4
Green beans (cooked)	1/2 cup	2.9
Jicama (raw)	1/2 cup	2.6
Cherry tomato	10, each	4.6
Scallions, chopped (raw)	1/2 cup	2.4
Turnip (cooked)	1/2 cup	2.4
Tomato, small (raw)	1, each	2.5
Portobello mushroom (cooked)	1, each	2.6
Kohlrabi (cooked)	1/2 cup	4.6
Brussel sprouts (cooked)	1/2 cup	3.5
Leeks (cooked)	2 TBSP	3.4
Tomato (cooked)	1/2 cup	8.6
Garlic, minced (raw)	2 TBSP	5.3
Cabbage (cooked)	1/2 cup	2.7
Pumpkin, mashed (cooked)	1/2 cup	4.7
Spaghetti squash (cooked)	1/2 cup	4
Yellow squash (cooked)	1/2 cup	2.6
Bell pepper, red, chopped (raw)	1/2 cup	3
Shallot, chopped (raw)	2 TBSP	3.4
Snow peas (cooked)	1/2 cup	5.4

Approximately 12 to 15 grams of Net Carbohydrates per day should be consumed from vegetables. Depending on the actual carb content, this is equal to several cups of the desired vegetable, where a cup is roughly the size of a baseball. Measure salad vegetables raw.

Salad Garnishes	SERVING SIZE	NET CARBS
Crumbled bacon	3 slices	0
Hard-boiled egg	1 egg	.5
Sautéed mushrooms	1/2 cup	1.0
Sour cream	2 Tbsp.	1.2

Salad Dressings	SERVING SIZE	NET CARBS
Red wine vinegar	1 TBSP	0
Caesar	2 TBSP	1
Ranch	2 TBSP	1.4
Lemon juice	2 TBSP	2.0
Bleu cheese	2 TBSP	2.3
Lime juice	2 TBSP	2.4
Balsamic vinegar	1 TBSP	2.7
Italian, creamy	2 TBSP	3

An acceptable salad dressing should have no added sugar and no more than 2 grams of Net Carbohydrates per serving (1-2 Tbsp)

Herbs and Spices	SERVING SIZE	NET CARBS
Basil	1 TBSP	0
Cayenne pepper	1 TBSP	0
Cilantro	1 TBSP	0
Dill	1 TBSP	0
Oregano	1 TBSP	0

Tarragon	1 TBSP	0
Parsley	1 TBSP	0.1
Chives (fresh or dehydrated)	1 TBSP	0.1
Ginger, fresh, grated	1 TBSP	0.8
Rosemary, dried	1 TBSP	0.8
Sage, ground	1 TSP	0.8
Black pepper	1 TSP	0.9
Garlic	1 clove	0.9

Make sure herbs and spices contain no added sugar.

All Fish Including:
- Sole, Tuna, Trout
- Cod, Flounder
- Herring, Salmon
- Sardines
- Halibut

All Shellfish Including:
- Clams
- Oysters*
- Shrimp
- Squid
- Crabmeat
- Mussels*
- Lobster

*No more than 4 ounces of oysters and mussels per day, due to their high carb counts.

All Meat Including:
- Ham*
- Lamb, Pork
- Bacon*
- Beef, Veal
- Venison

*Some meats will add to your carb count; these include processed meats such as bacon and sugar-cured ham. If possible, it is preferable to avoid meats with added nitrates, such as cold cuts.

All Poultry Including:
- Chicken, Duck
- Goose, Pheasant
- Cornish hen
- Quail, Turkey
- Ostrich

Eggs in Any Style, Including:
- Hard-boiled
- Deviled, Scrambled
- Fried, Omelette
- Poached, Soft-boiled

Eggs are a staple breakfast in the Atkins Nutritional Approach, due to their high nutritional value. A little creativity can do wonders for your egg-based breakfasts and snacks: add onions, mushrooms or green pepper. A topping of feta cheese, basil, oregano and other herbs can also add variation.

Fats and Oils
1. Mayonnaise – with no added sugar
2. Olive oil
3. Butter
4. Vegetable oils – Olive oil is one of the best, but varieties that are expeller-pressed or cold-pressed are also very good.
    - Sesame
    - Walnut
    - Sunflower*
    - Safflower*
    - Canola*
    - Soybean*
    - Grape seed*

*it is best to not let the temperature of these oils get too high. Olive oil should be used for sautéing only. Walnut and sesame oil should be used only for dressing cooked vegetables or salad.

Cheese	SERVING SIZE	NET CARBS
Parmesan, grated	1 Tbsp.	0.2
Goat or chèvre	1 oz.	0.3
Bleu cheeses	2 Tbsp.	0.4
Cheddar	1 oz.	0.4
Gouda	1 oz.	0.6
Mozzarella, whole milk	1 oz.	0.6
Cream cheese, whipped	2 Tbsp.	0.8
Parmesan, chunk	1 oz.	0.9
Swiss	1 oz.	1.0
Feta	1 oz.	1.2

It is worth noting that cheese does contain about 1 gram per ounce of carbohydrates. Eat no more than 3-4 ounces of cheese per day. An ounce is almost the size of an individually-wrapped slice of cheese or a 1" cube.

Beverages
- Bouillon/Clear broth (no added sugar)
- Diet soda (note the carb count)
- Flavored seltzer (zero calorie)
- Cream, heavy or light
- Herbal tea (no fruit sugar or barley added)
- Unflavored soy/almond milk
- Decaffeinated or regular coffee and tea*
- Club soda
- Water – at least 8-ounce glasses per day including:

	Filtered water, Mineral water, Tap water, Spring water
	* An individual may have one or two cups of coffee or caffeinated tea daily, according to their preference. Do not consume caffeine if symptoms of hypoglycemia or cravings are experienced as a result. The induction phase is best for breaking a caffeine addiction, should you suffer from one. * Consume no more than 3 T of lemon and lime juices per day * Consume no more than 3 TBSP or 1.5 fl. Oz. of cream (heavy or light) per day
Artificial Sweeteners	Sucralose, saccharine or stevia – one packet equals 1 gram of Net Carbohydrates
** If you have decided to stay in the Induction phase longer than 2 weeks, you may swap out 3g NC of other foundation vegetables for 3g NC of nuts or seeds. Do not let your Foundation Vegetable levels drop below 12g NC.	

Phase 2

Dairy	SERVING SIZE	NET CARBS
Mozzarella cheese	5 ounces	3.0
Yogurt, Greek	1/2 cup or 4 ounces	3.5
Ricotta cheese	1/2 cup	3.8
Cottage cheese, 2%	1/2 cup	4.1
Heavy cream	3/4 cup	4.8
Yogurt, Plain	1/2 cup or 4 ounces	5.5
Legumes (Cooked/Canned)	SERVING SIZE	NET CARBS
Lentils	1/4 cup	4
Kidney Beans	1/4 cup	5.9
Lima Beans	1/4 cup	6.1
Pinto Beans	1/4 cup	6.1
Black Beans	1/4 cup	6.5
Navy Beans	1/4 cup	10.1
Great Northern Beans	1/4 cup	10.6
Chickpeas	1/4 cup	10.9
Fruits	SERVING SIZE	NET CARBS
Blackberries (fresh)	1/4 cup	1.6
Raspberries (fresh)	1/4 cup	1.7
Cranberries (fresh)	1/4 cup	1.9
Strawberries, sliced (fresh)	1/4 cup	2.4
Cantaloupe, cubes	1/4 cup	2.9
Honeydew, cubes	1/4 cup	3.5
Gooseberries (fresh)	1/4 cup	3.9
Boysenberries (fresh)	1/4 cup	4.5
Blueberries (fresh)	1/4 cup	4.5
Juices	SERVING SIZE	NET CARBS
Lemon juice	2 TBSP	2.0
Lime juice	2 TBSP	2.4
Tomato juice	4 ounces	4.0

Nuts & Seeds (and Butters)	SERVING SIZE	NET CARBS
Brazil nuts	6 nuts	1.4
Macadamias	10 nuts	1.4
Hulled sunflower seeds	2 TBSP	1.5
Walnuts	12 nuts	1.7
Almonds	24 nuts	2.2
Pistachios	2 TBSP	3.0
Peanuts	2 TBSP	3.8
Pecans	2 TBSP	3.8
Cashews	2 TBSP	5.1

Convenience Foods

Many of the foods listed above are available in convenient "snack-size" packaging at the supermarket or convenience store; feel free to grab and go – just note the serving size, and subtract the fiber from total carbohydrates to get the total Net Carbohydrates.

Remember, Atkins bars and shakes are super convenient too, and every single flavor is allowed in Phase 2. So be busy, be happy and be well fed!

Phase 3

Grains*	SERVING SIZE	NET CARBS
Wheat bran (raw)	2 TBSP	1.6
Wheat germ	2 TBSP	4.9
Oat bran (raw)	2 TBSP	6.0
Quinoa (cooked)	1/4 cup	8.6
Whole wheat bread	1 slice	10
Oatmeal (dry, steel cut)	1/4 cup	11.5
Polenta (dry)	2 TBSP	12.5
Grits (cooked)	1/2 cup	15.2
Whole wheat pasta (cooked)	1/2 cup	16.6
Oatmeal (dry, rolled)	1/3 cup	19
Barley (cooked)	1/2 cup	19.2
Millet (cooked)	1/2 cup	19.5
Rice (brown, cooked)	1/2 cup	21.2

* Be sure to check the nutrition label for the most current NC count. Individual brands may vary.

Starchy Vegetables*	SERVING SIZE	NET CARBS
Carrots, sliced	1 medium	4.1
Rutabaga, cubed	1/2 cup	5.9
Beets, sliced	1/2 cup	6.8
Peas	1/2 cup	7
Acorn Squash (baked/mashed)	1/2 cup	7.6
Butternut squash	1/2 cup	8.5
Sweet potato, baked	1/2 medium	9.9
Parsnips, sliced	1/2 cup	10.2
Potato, baked	1/2 small	13.1
Corn	1/2 cup	14.9

Fruit	SERVING SIZE	NET CARBS
Coconut, fresh, shredded	1/2 cup	2.5
Figs, fresh	1 fruit	4.5

Cherries	1/4 cup	5.3
Watermelon, cubes	1/2 cup	5.5
Pomegranate seeds	1/4 cup	6.4
Papaya, pieces	1/2 cup	6.6
Plum, medium	1 fruit	6.6
Guava	1/2 cup	7.4
Clementine	1 fruit	7.6
Apple	1/2 fruit	7.9
Kiwi	1 fruit	8.1
Grapefruit (red)	1/2 fruit	8.9
Apricot, medium	3 fruits	9.6
Pineapple, fresh, chunks	1/2 cup	9.7
Peach, small	1 fruit	10.5
Mango	1/2 cup	11.1
Grapes (red)	1/2 cup	13
Orange, navel	1 fruit	14.5
Dates, fresh	3 fruits	15.8
Banana, small	1 fruit	20.4
Pear, medium	1 fruit	21

* All figures are for cooked (not raw) vegetables, legumes, or grains.

Phase 4

Grains	SERVING SIZE	NET CARBS
Wheat bran (raw)	2 TBSP	1.6
Wheat germ	2 TBSP	4.9
Oat bran (raw)	2 TBSP	6.0
Quinoa (cooked)	1/4 cup	8.6
Whole wheat bread	1 slice	10
Oatmeal (dry, steel cut)	1/4 cup	11.5
Polenta (dry)	2 TBSP	12.5
Grits (cooked)	1/2 cup	15.2
Whole wheat pasta (cooked)	1/2 cup	16.6
Oatmeal (dry, rolled)	1/3 cup	19
Barley (cooked)	1/2 cup	19.2
Millet (cooked)	1/2 cup	19.5
Rice (brown, cooked)	1/2 cup	21.2

*Be sure to check the nutrition label for the most current NC count. Individual brands may vary.

Starchy Vegetables	SERVING SIZE	NET CARBS
Carrots, sliced	1 medium	4.1
Rutabaga, sliced	1/2 cup	5.9
Beets, sliced	1/2 cup	6.8
Peas	1/2 cup	7
Acorn squash (cubed/mashed)	1/2 cup	7.6
Butternut squash	1/2 cup	8.5
Sweet potato, baked	1/2 medium	9.9
Parsnips, sliced	1/2 cup	10.2
Potato, baked	1/2 small	13.1

Corn	1/2 cup	14.9
Fruit	**SERVING SIZE**	**NET CARBS**
Coconut, fresh, shredded	1/2 cup	2.5
Figs, fresh	1 fruit	4.5
Cherries	1/4 cup	5.3
Watermelon, cubes	1/2 cup	5.5
Pomegranate seeds	1/4 cup	6.4
Papaya, pieces	1/2 cup	6.6
Plum, medium	1 fruit	6.6
Guava	1/2 cup	7.4
Clementine	1 fruit	7.6
Apple	1/2 fruit	7.9
Kiwi	1 fruit	8.1
Grapefruit (red)	1/2 fruit	8.9
Apricot, medium	3 fruits	9.6
Pineapple, fresh, chunks	1/2 cup	9.7
Peach, small	1 fruit	10.5
Mango	1/2 cup	11.1
Grapes (red)	1/2 cup	13
Orange, navel	1 fruit	14.5
Dates, fresh	3 fruits	15.8
Banana, small	1 fruit	20.4
Pear, medium	1 fruit	21

What Should I Avoid?

Foods other than those listed above are to be avoided.

Tips for Dining Out

1) To avoid overeating, have a light snack before going to a restaurant. Grab something light, like vegetables or turkey roll ups.
2) If you can't resist complimentary bread baskets or bowls of tortilla chips, you can politely ask your server to remove them. If your order of salsa, hummus or guacamole comes with chips or bread, ask if you can substitute sliced veggies instead.
3) Avoid high-carb options like fries, pasta salad or other high-carb sides. Ask for low-carb substitutes like asparagus or broccoli.
4) Avoid salads that come in shells (like tortilla) and go easy on the add-ons. Make sure that any meat in your salad is grilled, not breaded or fried. If you are in Phase 1, also avoid particularly high-carb fruits like grapes and mango.

5) Sandwich bread is a source of unnecessary carbohydrates; ask if your sandwich can be made into a salad or lettuce wrap. If not, limit yourself to the sandwich filling, or remove one slice for an open-faced option if you are in the later phases of Atkins.

Snack Choices

Try to keep your snacks healthy by making snacks out of any/all the foods previously listed in the chapter. Choose foods for your snack based on the phase of the Atkins diet that you are currently following. Also try to follow a routine or set number of snacks per day, for example 2 snacks a day. Make sure not to over-snack as that may be detrimental to your routine. Pack snacks in small containers or zip-top bags so you can track your intake of Net Carbohydrates. Here are some snacking options:

- Veggies with salad dressing
- Ham or turkey rollups
- Greek yogurt with berries
- Nuts, Olives
- Smoked salmon rolls
- Cheese, Hard-boiled eggs
- Atkins bars and shakes

Chapter 2: Everything About the Air Fryer

The air fryer is a modern kitchen gadget that uses the rapid circulation of hot air to cook foods through. If you are looking for healthy meals that are rich in texture, packed with flavor, nutrients, and low in fat, then using an air fryer would be the best choice. In this chapter, you will get to learn everything you need to know about air frying and how to use it as a professional.

What is An Air Fryer?

An air fryer is a one-of-a-kind conventional form of oven, almost the same size as a rice cooker. Cooking with an air fryer utilizes the rapid circulation of hot air around your meals (as the picture shows below). The circulation of heat moves at an incredibly high speed that it cooks quickly providing a crispy texture on the outside and a soft one the inside. Air fryers can fry, bake, roast, and grill any sorts of foods with the requirement of little to no oil at all.

Also, the air fryers have a timer and an adjustable temperature manager which means that you do not need to keep a tab on your food as everything is done automatically. Using an air fryer is a matter of adding the meal, adjusting the temperature, and setting the time. Although some recipes may require a little extra care, other than that, it's most often a times a pretty much smooth sailing experience whenever it comes to using the air fryers.

The Benefits of The Air Fryers

There is an endless list of benefits when it comes to air frying, and below are some of them:

1. Air fryers can provide you with delicious and tasty meals every day at any time.

2. Air fryers avoid dry fried foods (common in deep fryers), while at the same time retains the crispy texture on the outside.

3. Air fryers can cook and heat foods in a matter of minutes.

4. Air fryers is multiple purpose kitchen device as it can fry, grill, roast, bake, and even make soups.

5. Air fryers are user-friendly appliance that comes with a timer, which means that you can cook your food and walk away without any fear of oil splattering or spillages, grease fires, burning, or foods sticking.

6. Air fryers saves money as you will be using lesser oil to fry foods.

7. Air fryers are low-maintenance and easily cleaned devices as most parts can be stripped and dish washed.

8. Air fryers can prepare foods with eighty percent less fat than oil fried foods, thus making it much healthier.

9. Air fryers contains a lid for frying which makes it one of the safest devices that everyone could use in frying.

Air Fryer vs. Traditional Fryer

The major discrepancies between the traditional and air fryers include:

The Oil Factor: With an air fryer, it requires little to no oil, or in rare cases only a tablespoon or two at most cases, while on the other hand, deep fryers need a lot of oil. A deep fryer typically requires 1 to 4 quarts of cooking oil which also requires a constant oil replacement at certain intervals, meaning that you will spending more money on oil.

The Health Factor: With an air fryer, you will be using an unnoticeable percentage of oil, thus making it much healthier by reducing the fat content to 80 percent other than in the case of using a deep fryer.

The Neatness Factor: Air fryers have a dishwasher safe removable cooking component and is also easy to clean up. All that is required with an air fryer is to clean the cooking basket, cooking pan, and the drip pan which can all easily done by hand.

But in the case of using the deep fryers, oil vapors can settle on the counter top, kitchen walls, and even the floors, making it messy and detrimental to ones health. Thus, you will spend more time cleaning these surfaces. Also, cleaning the deep fryer is not easy, depending on the brand, some parts may or may not be safe to dish wash, and some areas may be impossible to reach.

The Safety Factor: Air frying is safe to use, because your cooking will be done while the food is covered with a lid. It can prepare foods without the need for you to stand beside it. However, when using a deep fryer, you need to stand in front of the hot oil to cook. Using the deep fryer carries more risk as the oil can splatter making the floors slippery, flickering on your skin, and even grease fire. Foods can also get burnt in the hot oil whereas with an air fryer you will just need to set the temperature, timer and walk away.

The Versatility Factor: Air fryers have multiple uses compared to the deep fryers. You can fry, grill, roast, and bake in your air fryers whereas you can use only deep fries in a deep fryer.

The Taste Factor: Deep fryers have a crunchier texture compared to the air fryers, because deep fryers are suitable for wet battered foods. In an air fryer, using wet batter foods will make the batter splatter, implying that to obtain a more crunchier texture, you will need to add an additional tablespoon of oil to your meals using an air fryer. The only difference would be the degree of crunchiness of the skin and of course the fat content.

The Time Factor: Deep frying is quicker than air frying. With deep fryers, heat is rapidly transferred from the hot oil to the food items. French fries will take around 10 to 15 minutes in your air fryer but only a couple of minutes in your deep fryer.

The Capacity Factor: Deep fryers generally have a large capacity than air fryers. If you are the type that cooks in large quantities (6+ servings), then deep fryers should be your most preferable. Air fryers is suitable for 2 to 4 servings at most.

The Reheating Factor: You can reheat foods in your air fryer in a matter of minutes compared to deep fryers. With deep fryers, it would not be so practical,because you will need to undergo the process of preparing the oil and cleaning afterward for just a small portion of food. Air fryers are more convenient and practical for reheating.

The Cost Factor: Air fryers are more costly than the deep fryers ranging from $50 to under $200 for the more expensive models. The air fryers cost more with most of the brands ranging from $100 to $200.

The Various Air Fryer Brands

Here is a list of some air fryer brands in the market. Find out which one is the best for you:

Phillips XL Air fryer: This air fryer has a large capacity making it a perfect choice for families or anyone who wishes to fry huge batches at once. This air fryer brand is also good for roasting, baking, and steaming ingredients. It comes with a dishwasher-safe for a smooth clean-up, a touch-screen interface, an adjustable temperature up to 390 degrees, and a 60-minute timer.

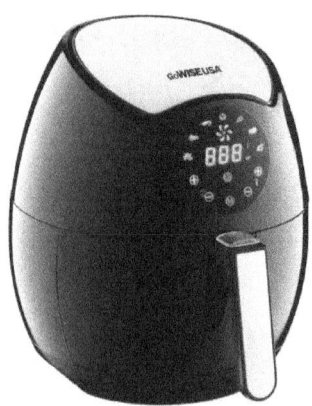

GoWISE USA GW22621 Electric Air Fryer: This brand has an adjustable temperature range of 175 to 390 degrees and can cook meals under 30 minutes. This air fryer is a practical choice for smaller families or for anyone who doesn't cook large batches frequently. The touchscreen is simple and has seven inbuilt programs. You can pick from the general food items including chips, chicken, fish, fries, and meat.

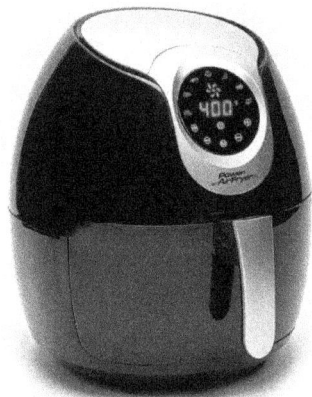

Power Air Fryer XL: This air fryer uses cyclonic heated air which cooks foods precisely and evenly for a delicious savory result without using any added oil. Other than that it comprises of an automated touch screen, and seven presets for popular meal items including chicken, fries, steaks, and baking goods.

Avalon Bay Digital Air Fryer: This brand comes with a fan that removes excess fats and oils from the food before air frying. The circulated air is then moved at a high speed to cook and heat the food efficiently for an even result. Also, this air fryer is perfect for baking, roasting, and grilling food items. The temperature for this brand ranges from 200 to 400 degrees and some customers claim you can use wet-battered ingredients with no expected splattering effects. It also has a non-slip rubber pad to hold the air fryer firmly in place.

NuWave Brio Air Fryer: This air fryer is good for cooking foods faster and simpler. This brand comes with of a preheat function, which brings the fryer to the best possible cooking temperature for your foods. It also has a digital touch screen to adjust the temperature and time. Also in this brand to ensure safety, the air frying process won't begin until the fry bucket is fully locked.

How to Use an Air Fryer

There are 4 steps in using an air fryer, follow this set of instructions when cooking anything with it:

Preparation: To prevent ingredients from sticking to the air fryer basket, spray it with a nonstick cooking spray or add a tablespoon of oil. Don't over pack foods in your air fryer basket otherwise some parts won't be fully cooked thoroughly. If you are working with a marinated or wet ingredients, make sure you rub them dry, because this will help avert splattering or excess smoke.

Pre-Heating: Plug in your air fryer and preheat it. This usually takes around five minutes, although preheating is not that necessary, nevertheless it can reduce your time in cooking.

Cooking: If you are cooking frozen foods or items with small ingredients, try shaking the air fryer many times to prepare it evenly and efficiently. Also when cooking high fatty foods, you should have it at the back of your mind that ,the fats will drop to the base of the air fryer, which will thereafter need cleaning.

Cleaning: To ensure your air fryer stays in shape, make sure you clean it properly by purifying the air fryer basket and the pan after using them. Most air fryers come with dishwasher safe parts which makes this process easy.

How to Clean & Maintain An Air Fryer

The first thing you should have at your finger tips is that, if you do not clean and maintain your air fryer from time to time, it won't last long. Following these guidelines will secure the fact that your air fryer will remain effective and durable for years to come.

How to clean your air fryer

Unplug your air fryer from the wall socket and allow it to cool until you can touch.

Using a wet rag, wipe the exterior part of your air fryer.

Remove the air fryer pan, tray, basket and wash it with hot water and a dishwasher soap in your sink. These parts are removable and are safe for an easy cleanup.

Use a cloth or sponge to wipe and clean the inner part of your air fryer.

If you find any ingredients sticking in your air fryer, scrub it off with a brush.

Before adding the pan, tray, and basket back into your air fryer ensure they are entirely dry.

Once your air fryer is cleaned, store it safely.

How to maintain your air fryer

Your air fryer requires a standard form of maintenance to ensure it does not get damaged or work erroneously. To do this, one needs to follow this instructions:

Before using your air fryer, make sure you check the cord. That is, do not plug a damaged cord into an outlet; this can result in a ghastly injury or even death.

Make sure your air fryer is clean and free of any debris before you begin cooking. Check the inner part and make sure you remove anything redundant in there.

Ensure the air fryer is placed upright, on a flat surface.

Make sure that your air fryer is not too close to the wall or another appliance. Air fryers require 4-inches of space all around them.

One after the other, check each component of your air fryer, including the basket, pan, and handle.

If you find anything damaged or wrong with your air fryer, reach the manufacturer and get it replaced.

How to Choose a Good Air Fryer

There are wide varieties of air fryers available to you. The smartest choice will be to purchase from popular brands like Phillips, Kalorik, or some special air fryer brands recommended by experts and professionals. Here is some more insight when it comes to ordering your air fryer.

What affects the buyer's decision of your air fryer?
The increasing revenue of air fryers has reaped from its benefits of making healthy and low-cholesterol meals. With this you can cook fried chicken and potato chips

that are healthy, nutritious, and less toxic than those of traditionally fried foods. Other benefits of air frying include fast cooking and an easy to use interface that it presents in your kitchen. With all this, who wouldn't buy an air fryer?

Tips on how to choose the air fryer best for you.

When it comes to owning an air fryer, there are some things you should have in in mind:

The size of your air fryer: The perfect sized air fryer gives your kitchen an enough space to serve, cook, and eat. To figure out the right size, you should have in mind that the ordinary air fryer can accommodate around 1.5 to 2 pounds of food items.

The capacity of your air fryer: Air fryers are electrically operated. Hence, inconsistencies in wattage stock can spark damage and electric shocks in your kitchen. Most standard ranges of air fryer capacity are from 700 to 1500 watts.

Controlling and signaling points: A good air fryer should have a digital touchscreen interface that can adjust temperature and time as well as switch modes. A timer is required to ensure fast and safe cooking. Some additional features should be checked for as it is going to give more comfort throughout your day to day cooking.

Warranty: Like any other device, buying gadgets will be more valuable due to its concentrated and considerate warranty terms. Having a warranty on your air fryer will be better than buying an air fryer without one. It is also preferable to purchase air fryers with full package home delivery.

The cost of your air fryer: Though an air fryer is highly recommended, it is costly compared to other kitchen gadgets. This is because of its level of utility as it prevents any form of grease fires, burns, and injury. The cost of air fryers is the most challenging factor for many and as such it is advisable that you should choose types that will lie within the whims and caprices of your budget.

It is also important to know that no matter the brand or price, all air fryers perform the same task irrespective. They all follow the principle of circulating hot air to cook and heat foods together. And so, your choice of an air fryer should not depend on technology or functions, but on the points mentioned above. Quality air fryers last longer and serve your needs better than investing in a cheaper module.

Where to Buy a Good Air Fryer?

There are many ways you can purchase an air fryer. Once you decide on the brand, you can Google and search up their websites. Alternatively, you can purchase air fryers on Amazon, online stores, and even grocery stores in their kitchen appliances section.

Air Frying Compatible Foods

Here is a list of compatible Air Frying foods:

Frozen Foods: Any kind of frozen foodstuff intended for baking purposes is a perfect fit for the air fryer. frozen things like fries, nuggets, and fish sticks cooks faster in your air fryer compared to your oven. And since there is no oil involved, it will lead to a low calories meal. For instance, French fries take around 12 minutes to achieve the crispy texture on the outside and a soft texture on the inside. You can shake the foods halfway through to ensure proper cooking and browning.

Raw Meat: You can roast any sort of meat in your air fryer, whether chicken, steak, pork, lamb, etc. A whole chicken will typically take about half an hour at 360 degrees F. to get done.

Vegetables: You can cook almost all forms of vegetables in your air fryer. Vegetables that you would normally grill can be done in your air fryer, and these includes cauliflower, green beans, onions, bell peppers can be all grilled in your air fryer.

Baked Goods: You can buy a nonstick baking dish along with your air fryer which is very useful when it comes to baking muffins, bread, lasagna, quiche, small cakes, or any other baked goods. This means you can bake anything you usually do in your oven using your air fryer with a more quicker and effective experience.

Roasting Nuts: Roasting nuts such as peanuts, walnuts, almonds, or any other kind of nuts can be easily done in your air fryer. This process will only take about 5 to 8 minutes, without it getting burned.

Wet-Battered Foods: Wet battered food is not suitable for air frying. The reason behind this is because the fast-moving air will burst the batter away from the food, causing it to splatter all over the cook basket, and creating a huge mess.

FAQs of Air Fryer

1. Can we cook various kinds of food in the air fryer?
Yes, you can easily prepare and cook any variety of foods in your air fryer. You can easily cook meats, potatoes, poultry, onion rings, and chicken nuggets .Aside from these things you can also bake cupcakes and grill vegetables.

2. How long does it take to cook frozen foods?
One of the great things about air frying frozen food is that it allows you to use the handle. But it usually takes more time to cook frozen foods compared to fresh ingredients.

3. How much can I cook in my air fryer?
This answer depends on the capacity of your air fryer. The majority of air fryers can hold up to 500 grams of food items. You can also see the max line of the basket on the air fryer which implies that the air fryer can be loaded up to that line.

4. Is there any specific kind of oils needed for air frying?
No, you don't need any special kind of oil for air frying. At most some recipes require a tablespoon or two of oil, of which you can use olive oil, coconut oil, vegetable oil, or butter spray.

5. Can I add more ingredients while the food is getting cooked in my air fryer?
Yes, you can add more ingredients while the food is getting cooked in your air fryer. However, be sure that the ingredients are added in the right away or else you may lose the heat which will result in an increase in the to cooking time.

6. Can I use a baking paper or aluminum foil in my air fryer?
Yes, you can use baking paper or aluminum foil, but you need to allocate some breathing space so that the steam can flow smoothly.

7. Is preheating required before I cook?

No, there is no need to preheat your air fryer. However, if you decide to preheat, it will take around 3 to 4 minutes and can help reduce the cooking time.

Now that we have known everything about the air fryer, let's cook some tasty and easy-to-make meals. It's effortless, all you have to do is just to follow the instructions properly. Also, do keep in mind that you are free to adjust the the recipes to your liking.

Chapter 3: Air Fryer Breakfast Recipes

Delicious Breakfast Souffle

Time: 20 minutes

Yield: 4

Ingredients:

- 6 eggs
- 1/3 of cup of milk
- ½ cup of shredded mozzarella cheese
- 1 tablespoon of freshly chopped parsley
- ½ cup of chopped ham
- 1 teaspoon of salt
- 1 teaspoon of black pepper
- ½ teaspoon of garlic powder

Instructions:

1. Grease 4 ramekins with a nonstick cooking spray.
2. Preheat your air fryer to 350 degrees Fahrenheit.
3. Using a large bowl, add and stir all the ingredients until it mixes properly.
4. Pour the egg mixture into the greased ramekins and place it inside your air fryer.
5. Cook it inside your air fryer for 8 minutes.
6. Then carefully remove the souffle from your air fryer and allow it to cool off.
7. Serve and enjoy!

Nutritional Information per serving:

Calories: 195, Fat: 15g, Protein: 9g, Carbohydrates: 6g, Dietary Fiber: 0.1g

Yummy Breakfast Italian Frittata

Time: 15 minutes

Yield: 4

Ingredients:

- 6 eggs
- 1/3 cup of milk
- 4-ounces of chopped Italian sausage
- 3 cups of stemmed and roughly chopped kale
- 1 red deseeded and chopped bell pepper
- ½ cup of a grated feta cheese
- 1 chopped zucchini
- 1 tablespoon of freshly chopped basil
- 1 teaspoon of garlic powder
- 1 teaspoon of onion powder
- 1 teaspoon of salt
- 1 teaspoon of black pepper

Instructions:

1. Preheat your air fryer to 360 degrees Fahrenheit.
2. Grease the air fryer pan with a nonstick cooking spray.
3. Add the Italian sausage to the pan and cook it inside your air fryer for 5 minutes.
4. While doing that, add and stir in the remaining ingredients until it mixes properly.
5. Add the egg mixture to the pan and allow it to cook inside your air fryer for 5 minutes.
6. Thereafter carefully remove the pan and allow it to cool off until it gets chill enough to serve.
7. Serve and enjoy!

Nutritional Information per serving:

Calories: 225, Fat: 14g, Protein: 20g, Dietary Fiber: 0.8g, Carbohydrates: 4.5g

Savory Cheese and Bacon Muffins

Time: 22 minutes

Yield: 4

Ingredients:

- 1 ½ cup of all-purpose flour
- 2 teaspoons of baking powder
- ½ cup of milk
- 2 eggs
- 1 tablespoon of freshly chopped parsley
- 4 cooked and chopped bacon slices
- 1 thinly chopped onion
- ½ cup of shredded cheddar cheese
- ½ teaspoon of onion powder
- 1 teaspoon of salt
- 1 teaspoon of black pepper

Instructions:

1. Preheat your air fryer to 360 degrees Fahrenheit.
2. Using a large bowl, add and stir all the ingredients until it mixes properly.
3. Then grease the muffin cups with a nonstick cooking spray or line it with a parchment paper. Pour the batter proportionally into each muffin cup.
4. Place it inside your air fryer and bake it for 15 minutes.
5. Thereafter, carefully remove it from your air fryer and allow it to chill.
6. Serve and enjoy!

Nutritional Information per serving:

Calories: 180, Fat: 18g, Protein: 15g, Dietary Fiber: 0.7g, Carbohydrates: 16g

Best Air-Fried English Breakfast

Time: 25 minutes

Yield: 4

Ingredients:

- 8 sausages
- 8 bacon slices
- 4 eggs
- 1 (16-ounce) can of baked beans
- 8 slices of toast

Instructions:

1. Add the sausages and bacon slices to your air fryer and cook them for 10 minutes at a 320 degrees Fahrenheit.
2. Using a ramekin or heat-safe bowl, add the baked beans, then place another ramekin and add the eggs and whisk.
3. Increase the temperature to 290 degrees Fahrenheit.
4. Place it inside your air fryer and cook it for an additional 10 minutes or until everything is done.
5. Serve and enjoy!

Nutritional Information per serving:

Calories: 850, Fat: 40g, Protein: 48g, Dietary Fiber: 18g,

Carbohydrates: 20g

Chapter 4: Air Fryer Lunch Recipes

Incredible Air-Fried Burgers

Time: 45 minutes

Yield: 4

Ingredients:

- 1 pound of lean ground beef
- 1 teaspoon of salt
- 1 teaspoon of black pepper
- 1 teaspoon of onion powder
- 1 teaspoon of garlic powder
- 1 tablespoon of freshly chopped or dried parsley
- 1 tablespoon of Worcestershire sauce

Instructions:

1. Preheat your air fryer to 390 degrees Fahrenheit.
2. Using a large bowl, add and mix all the ingredients until it is properly mixed.
3. Grease your air fryer cooking tray with a nonstick cooking spray.
4. Segment the ground beef mixture into four medium-sized patties and place it in the tray.
5. Place the tray inside your air fryer and cook it for 25 minutes.
6. After 25 minutes, flip the burgers and cook it for an additional 20 minutes.
7. Then gather your burgers and add any toppings you like.
8. Serve and enjoy!

Nutritional Information per serving:

Calories: 148, Fat: 5g, Protein: 24g, Dietary Fiber: 0.3g,

Carbohydrates: 1.7g

Extraordinary Stuffed Zucchini with Bacon and Jalapeno

Time: 15 minutes

Yield: 2

Ingredients:

- 3 zucchinis
- 6 cooked and crumbled bacon slices
- 1 chopped jalapeno
- 2 chopped tomatoes
- 1 (8-ounce) can of tomato sauce
- 1 cup of shredded mozzarella cheese
- 1 tablespoon of freshly chopped parsley
- 1 teaspoon of salt
- 1 teaspoon of black pepper

Instructions:

1. Cut the zucchini vertically and scoop out the inner portions.
2. Using a large bowl, add and mix the bacon, jalapeno, salt, black pepper, the parsley properly.
3. Pour in the tomatoes, the tomato sauce and stir until it mixes properly.
4. Fill the zucchini with the ground beef mixture and sprinkle it with the cheese
5. Place the stuffed zucchini in your air fryer basket and cook it for 10 minutes.
6. Serve and enjoy!

Nutritional Information per serving:

Calories: 210, Fat: 8g, Protein: 23g, Dietary Fiber: 2g,

Carbohydrates: 6g

Good-Tasting Turkey Rolls

Time: 40 minutes

Yield: 4

Ingredients:

- 2 tortilla wraps
- 2 cups of shredded leftover turkey breast
- 2 eggs
- 1 tablespoon of honey
- 1 tablespoon of soy sauce
- 1 tablespoon of Chinese five-spice
- 1 teaspoon of Worcester sauce
- 1 teaspoon of salt
- 1 teaspoon of black pepper

Instructions:

1. Using a bowl, add the shredded leftover turkey breasts and seasonings. Mix it with your washed hands until it mixes properly.
2. Roll out the tortilla wraps thinly and avoid breaking or cracking any tortillas.
3. Using a bowl, add and beat the eggs.
4. Brush the egg wash on both sides and allow it to refrigerate for 30 minutes.
5. After thirty minutes, remove the tortilla wraps and cut it into 8 spring roll sheets.
6. Fill the shredded leftover turkey into each sheet.
7. Roll each turkey into a spring roll and brush it with the egg wash.
8. Place it inside your air fryer and cook it for 5 minutes at a 360 degrees Fahrenheit.

Nutritional Information per serving:

Calories: 45, Fat: 2g, Protein: 5g, Dietary Fiber: 0g,

Carbohydrates: 0.2g

Chapter 5: Air Fryer Dinner Recipes

General Wong's Beef and Broccoli

Time: 25 minutes (plus 30 minutes for marinating)

Yield: 4

Ingredients:

- 1 pound of steak, sliced into strips
- 1 pound of stemmed and chopped into florets broccoli
- 1/3 cup of oyster sauce
- 1/3 cup of sherry
- 1 tablespoon of minced ginger
- 1 tablespoon of minced garlic
- 1 tablespoon of olive oil
- 1 tablespoon of soy sauce
- 1 tablespoon of sesame oil
- 1 teaspoon of cornstarch

Instructions:

1. Using a bowl, add the oyster sauce, sherry, minced ginger, minced garlic, olive oil, soy sauce, sesame oil, cornstarch and stir it until it is properly mixed.
2. Then, add the steak, broccoli, cover it well and allow it to marinate for 30 minutes or overnight.
3. Then preheat your air fryer to 360 degrees Fahrenheit.
4. After marinating, place the marinade steak and broccoli in your air fryer.
5. Cook it for 15 minutes at a 360 degrees Fahrenheit or until it is done.
6. Serve and enjoy along with the white rice!

Nutritional Information per serving:

Calories: 340, Fat: 21g, Protein: 21g, Dietary Fiber: 2.5g, Carbohydrates: 18g

Irresistible Meatloaf

Time: 25 minutes

Yield: 4

Ingredients:

- 1 ½ pound of lean ground beef
- 1 beaten egg
- 1 cup of panko breadcrumbs
- 1/3 cup of steak sauce
- 1 finely chopped onion
- 1 chopped green bell pepper
- ½ cup of chopped mushrooms
- 1 tablespoon of chopped thyme
- 1 teaspoon of paprika
- 1 teaspoon of garlic powder
- 1 teaspoon of salt
- 1 teaspoon of black pepper

Instructions:

1. Preheat your air fryer to 390 degrees Fahrenheit.
2. Using a large bowl, add all the ingredients and stir until it mixes properly.
3. Thereafter, grease a heat-safe pan or the air fryer baking accessory with a nonstick cooking spray.
4. Add the mixed ground beef into the pan or baking accessory and flatten the top.
5. After that, place the pan or accessory inside your air fryer and cook it for 25 minutes at a 390 degrees Fahrenheit or until it gets brown and done.
6. Thereafter, carefully remove it from your air fryer and allow it to cool off before serving.
7. Serve and enjoy!

Nutritional Information per serving:

Calories: 300, Fat: 18g, Protein: 23g, Dietary fiber: 0.7g, Carbohydrates: 9g

Rockstar Rib Eye-Steak

Time: 20 minutes

Yield: 1 or 2

Ingredients:

- 2 pounds of rib-eye steak
- 1 tablespoon of olive oil
- 1 teaspoon of salt
- 1 teaspoon of black pepper
- 1 teaspoon of ground coriander
- 1 teaspoon of brown sugar
- 1 teaspoon of sweet paprika
- 1 teaspoon of mustard powder
- 1 teaspoon of onion powder
- 1 teaspoon of chili powder
- 1 teaspoon of garlic powder

Instructions:

1. Preheat your air fryer to 390 degrees Fahrenheit.
2. Sprinkle the olive oil over the rib-eye steak.
3. Season the steak on all sides with all the listed seasonings until it is well covered.
4. Place the steak into your air fryer basket.
5. Cook it for 8 minutes at a 390 degrees Fahrenheit.
6. After 8 minutes, flip the steak over and cook for an additional 7 minutes.
7. When done, carefully remove the steak from your air fryer and allow it to cool off before serving.
8. Serve and enjoy!

Nutritional Information per serving:

Calories: 520, Fat: 35g, Dietary Fiber: 0g, Carbohydrates: 2g, Protein: 56g

Super-Yummy Roast Pork Belly

Time:

Yield: 2

Ingredients:

- 2 pounds of pork belly
- 2 teaspoons of garlic powder
- 2 teaspoons of onion powder
- 1 teaspoon of smoked paprika
- 1 teaspoon of salt
- 2 teaspoons of five-spice powder
- 2 teaspoons of rosemary
- 1 teaspoon of black pepper

Instructions:

1. Fill a large pot with enough water, boil it and then add the pork belly into the hot water for 10 minutes.
2. Then remove it from the boiling water and allow it to dry for 3 hours or until it dries completely.
3. Use a fork to poke some holes all around the pork belly.
4. While still doing that, using a small mixing bowl, add and mix all the seasonings together, then rub the pork belly with the seasonings.
5. Preheat your air fryer to 320 degrees Fahrenheit.
6. Place the pork belly inside your air fryer and cook it for 30 minutes.
7. Increase the temperature to 360 degrees Fahrenheit and cook it for an additional 20 minutes.
8. Serve and enjoy!

Nutritional Information per serving:

Calories: 240, Fat: 20g, Protein: 13g, Dietary Fiber: 0g, Carbohydrates: 1g

Outstanding Rack of Lamb

Time: 25 minutes

Yield: 4

Ingredients:

- 2 racks of lamb
- ¼ cup of freshly chopped parsley
- 4 cloves of minced garlic
- 2 tablespoons of olive oil
- 2 tablespoons of honey
- 1 teaspoon of salt
- 1 teaspoon of black pepper

Instructions:

1. Preheat your air fryer to 390 degrees Fahrenheit.
2. Using a blender or food processor, add the parsley, garlic cloves, olive oil, honey, salt, and black pepper and blend it until it gets totally grounded.
3. Rub the grounded parsley-garlic on the lamb racks, without using them all as you will need them later.
4. Put the grill pan accessory into your air fryer, and place the lamb racks on top.
5. Cook it for 15 minutes at a 390 degrees Fahrenheit or until it gets brown in color.
6. Spread another layer of the puree on the lamb racks.
7. Serve and enjoy!

Nutritional Information per serving:

Calories: 335, Fat: 26g, Protein: 21g, Dietary Fiber: 0g, Carbohydrates: 2.5g

Phenomenal Herbed Roast Beef

Time: 1 hour

Yield: 4

Ingredients:

- 4-pound roasted beef
- 1 tablespoon of olive oil
- 1 teaspoon of salt
- 1 teaspoon of black pepper
- 1 teaspoon of dried thyme
- 1 tablespoon of freshly chopped rosemary
- 1 tablespoon of freshly chopped parsley

Instructions:

1. Preheat your air fryer to 360 degrees Fahrenheit.
2. Using a bowl, add and mix the olive oil, salt, black pepper, thyme, rosemary, parsley properly.
3. Rub the mixture all over the roasted beef.
4. Place the beef inside your air fryer basket and cook it for 20 minutes.
5. After 20 minutes, flip the beef over and cook for an additional 30 minutes or until it reaches your desired preference.
6. Remove the roasted beef and allow it to cool of before serving.
7. Serve and enjoy!

Nutritional Information per serving:

Calories: 210, Fat: 10g, Protein: 27g, Dietary Fiber: 0.2g, Carbohydrates: 0.6g

Amazing Lamb Chops with Herbed Garlic Sauce

Time: 25 minutes

Yield: 4

Ingredients:

- 4 lamb chops
- 1 garlic bulb
- 1 tablespoon of freshly chopped parsley
- 1 tablespoon of freshly chopped oregano
- 2 tablespoons of olive oil
- 1 teaspoon of onion powder
- 1 teaspoon of salt
- 1 teaspoon of black pepper

Instructions:

1. Preheat your air fryer to 390 degrees Fahrenheit.
2. Brush the garlic bulb with an olive oil and place it inside your air fryer, cook it for 12 minutes or until it is properly roasted, then remove it from your air fryer and set it aside.
3. Using a small bowl, mix the parsley, oregano, olive oil, onion powder, salt, and the black pepper properly.
4. Thereafter spread each lamb chop with about one teaspoon of the herbed olive oil mixture.
5. Place the lamb chops into your air fryer and cook it for 6 minutes at a 390 degrees Fahrenheit or until it turns brown.
6. Press the garlic cloves with a garlic press and mix it properly with the herbed olive oil.
7. Spread the garlic sauce over the lamb chops.
8. Serve and enjoy!

Nutritional Information per serving:

Calories: 180, Fat: 8g, Protein: 23g, Carbohydrates: 1.7g, Dietary Fiber: 0.5g

Chapter 6: Air Fryer Appetizer Recipes

Astonishing Chicken Kebabs

Time: 15 minutes

Yield: 2

Ingredients:

- 2 chopped boneless, skinless chicken breasts
- 6 halves of mushrooms
- 1 chopped red bell pepper
- 1 chopped green bell pepper
- 1 chopped yellow bell pepper
- 1/3 cup of honey
- 1/3 cup of soy sauce
- 1 teaspoon of salt
- 1 teaspoon of black pepper
- Wooden skewers

Instructions:

1. Preheat your air fryer to 340 degrees Fahrenheit.
2. Using a bowl, add and mix 1/3 cup of honey, 1/3 cup of soy sauce, salt, and black pepper.
3. For each wooden skewer, add the bell peppers, chicken, and mushroom slices.
4. Thereafter, brush the chicken kabobs with the honey soy sauce mixture.
5. Place the chicken kabobs into your air fryer basket and cook it for 15 to 20 minutes.
6. Serve and enjoy!

Nutritional Information per serving:

Calories: 90, Fat: 14g, Protein: 8g, Dietary Fiber: 1g, Carbohydrates: 6g

Appetizing Avocado Fries

Time: 20 minutes

Yield: 4

Ingredients:

- 2 avocados, peeled, pitted, and sliced into fries
- 1 cup of panko breadcrumbs
- 1 teaspoon of salt

Instructions:

1. Preheat your air fryer to 390 degrees Fahrenheit.
2. Using a bowl, mix the panko breadcrumbs with 1 teaspoon of salt.
3. Dredge the avocado fries into the panko breadcrumb mixture until it is properly covered.
4. Place the avocado fries inside your air fryer, cook it for 10 minutes and then shake it 5 minutes after that.
5. Serve and enjoy!

Nutritional Information per serving:

Calories: 130, Fat: 11g, Protein: 4g, Dietary Fiber: 4g, Carbohydrates: 6g

Godly Pork Taquitos

Time: 25 minutes

Yield: 4

Ingredients:

- 30-ounces of cooked and shredded pork tenderloin
- 2 ½ cups of shredded mozzarella cheese
- 10 small whole wheat tortillas
- 1 lime juice

Instructions:

1. Preheat your air fryer to 380 degrees Fahrenheit.
2. Stir the lime juice over the shredded pork tenderloins.
3. Soften the tortillas in your air fryer by microwaving it for 10 seconds.
4. For each tortilla add 3-ounces of the shredded pork and ¼ cup of the mozzarella cheese.
5. lightly roll up the tortillas.
6. Then spray a nonstick cooking spray over the tortillas and place it inside your air fryer.
7. Cook it for 7 to 10 minutes or until it gets a golden brown color, and then flip after 5 minutes.
8. Serve and enjoy!

Nutritional Information per serving:

Calories: 210, Fat: 29g, Protein: 7g, Dietary Fiber: 3g, Carbohydrates: 15g

Gratifying Stuffed Mushrooms

Time: 35 minutes

Yield: 2

Ingredients:

- 6 mushrooms
- ½ cup of peeled and chopped onion
- 1 tablespoon of breadcrumbs
- 1 teaspoon of garlic puree
- 1 tablespoon of olive oil
- 1 teaspoon of freshly chopped parsley
- 1 teaspoon of salt
- 1 teaspoon of black pepper

Instructions:

1. Using a bowl, add the onion, breadcrumbs, garlic puree, olive oil, parsley, salt, and black pepper.
2. Remove the middle stalk of each mushroom and fill them with the onion mixture.
3. Grease your air fryer basket and place the stuffed mushrooms into it.
4. Cook it for 10 minutes at a 360 degrees Fahrenheit.
5. Once done, carefully remove it from your air fryer and cook it for 10 minutes.
6. Serve and enjoy!

Nutritional Information per serving:

Calories: 80, Fat; 7g, Protein: 6g, Carbohydrates: 5g, Dietary Fiber: 2.5g

Everyday Chicken Nuggets

Time: 17 minutes

Yield: 2

Ingredients:

- 1 pound of boneless, skinless chicken breasts, cut into 1-inch pieces
- 1 beaten egg
- 1 cup of milk
- 2 cups of flour
- 1 cup of breadcrumbs
- 2 teaspoons of salt
- 1 teaspoon of black pepper
- 1 teaspoon of sweet paprika

Instructions:

1. Preheat your air fryer to 360 degrees Fahrenheit.
2. Using a bowl, mix the eggs and milk properly.
3. Pick a second bowl, add the flour and place it aside.
4. Then using a third bowl, add the breadcrumbs, salt, black pepper, sweet paprika and mix properly.
5. Dredge the chicken pieces in the flour, soak the chicken pieces into the egg wash, and then cover it with the seasoned breadcrumbs.
6. Place the chicken pieces in your air fryer and cook it for 10 minutes at a 360 degrees Fahrenheit or until it has a golden brown color, flipping halfway through.
7. Serve and enjoy!

Nutritional Information per serving:

Calories: 190, Fat: 9g, Protein: 7g, Dietary Fiber: 1g, Carbohydrates: 20g

Chapter 7: Air Fryer Poultry Recipes

Flavorful Fried Chicken

Time: 30 minutes

Yield: 4

Ingredients:

- 4 small chicken thighs
- 1 cup of flour
- 1 cup of breadcrumbs
- 2 beaten eggs
- 1 teaspoon of salt
- 1 tablespoon of Cajun seasoning

Instructions:

1. Preheat your air fryer to 390 degrees Fahrenheit.
2. Using three bowls, add the flour to the first bowl, in the second bowl add the eggs and beat it properly, and in the third bowl add the breadcrumbs, salt, Cajun seasoning and mix properly.
3. Dredge the chicken thighs in the flour, immerse it into the egg mixture, and cover it with the breadcrumbs.
4. Grease your air fryer basket with a nonstick cooking spray and put in the 4 chicken thighs inside.
5. Cook it for 25 minutes until the chicken is crispy and turns golden brown.
6. Serve and enjoy!

Nutritional Information per serving:

Calories: 200, Fat: 22g, Protein: 19g, Dietary Fiber: 0g, Carbohydrates: 19g

Delectable Whole Roast Chicken

Time: 50 minutes

Yield: 4

Ingredients:

- 1 (4-pound) whole chicken
- 1 tablespoon of olive oil
- 1 teaspoon of salt
- 1 teaspoon of black pepper
- 1 teaspoon of paprika
- 1 teaspoon of onion powder
- 1 teaspoon of garlic powder
- 1 teaspoon of Italian seasoning
- 1 teaspoon of brown sugar
- 1 tablespoon of dried thyme
- 1 tablespoon of dried oregano
- 1 tablespoon of cayenne pepper

Instructions:

1. Preheat your air fryer to 340 degrees Fahrenheit.
2. Sprinkle the whole chicken with olive oil and rub the seasoning all over.
3. Grease your air fryer basket with a nonstick cooking spray and add the chicken to it.
4. Cook the chicken inside your air fryer for 30 minutes at a 340 degrees Fahrenheit.
5. After 30 minutes, flip the chicken and cook it for an additional 20 minutes or until it is totally done.
6. Serve and enjoy!

Nutritional Information per serving:

Calories: 155, Fat: 3.8g, Dietary Fiber: 0g, Carbohydrates: 0g, Protein: 28g

Divine Buffalo Wings

Time: 25 minutes (plus 4 hours of marinating time)

Yield: 4

Ingredients:

- 2 pounds of chicken wings
- 3 tablespoons of melted butter
- ¼ cup of hot sauce
- 1 teaspoon of paprika
- 1 teaspoon of cayenne pepper
- 1 teaspoon of salt
- 1 teaspoon of black pepper

Buffalo Sauce Ingredients:

- 3 tablespoons of melted butter
- ¼ cup of hot sauce

Instructions:

1. Using a separate bowl, add 3 tablespoons of melted butter, ¼ cup of hot sauce, paprika, cayenne pepper, salt, black pepper, chicken wings and allow it to marinate for 4 hours or overnight.
2. Preheat your air fryer to 390 degrees Fahrenheit.
3. Lubricate your air fryer basket with a nonstick cooking spray and add half of the chicken wings.
4. Cook the chicken wings for 14 minutes, then shake it 7 minutes after and repeat this with the other batch.
5. Using another bowl, add 3 tablespoons of melted butter and ¼ cup of hot sauce.
6. Remove the chicken wings from your air fryer and combine it with the buffalo sauce.
7. Serve and enjoy!

Nutritional Information per serving:

Calories: 240, Fat: 15.5g, Protein: 8g, Carbohydrates: 5g, Dietary Fiber: 6g

Flavorsome Honey Lime Chicken Wings

Time: 30 minutes

Yield: 4

Ingredients:

- 2 pounds of chicken wings
- ¼ cup of honey
- 2 tablespoons of lime juice
- 1 tablespoon of lime
- 1 pressed clove of garlic
- 1 teaspoon of salt
- 1 teaspoon of black pepper

Instructions:

1. Preheat your air fryer to 360 degrees Fahrenheit.
2. Using a bowl, mix the honey, lime juice, lime zest, garlic clove, salt, and black pepper.
3. Add the chicken wings and toss it until it is well covered with the honey-lime mixture.
4. Working in batches, add half of the chicken wings into the air fryer.
5. Cook it for 25 to 30 minutes or until it turns golden brown and crispy, while shaking it every 8 minutes.
6. Serve and enjoy!

Nutritional Information per serving:

Calories: 280, Fat: 25g, Dietary Fiber: 0.2g, Carbohydrates: 3.6g, Protein: 23g

Delightful Coconut Crusted Chicken Tenders

Time: 30 minutes

Yield: 4

Ingredients:

- 1 pound of chicken tender
- 3 beaten eggs
- 2 cups of sweetened shredded coconut
- 1 cup of cornstarch
- 1 teaspoon of salt
- 1 teaspoon of black pepper
- 1 teaspoon of cayenne pepper

Instructions:

1. Preheat your air fryer to 360 degrees Fahrenheit.
2. Using three bowls, add the cornstarch, salt, black pepper, and cayenne pepper into the first bowl. Then in the second bowl, add the eggs and beat it until it mixes properly. While in the third bowl, add the shredded coconut.
3. Dredge each chicken tender in the cornstarch mixture, then dip it into the egg wash, and then cover it with the shredded coconut.
4. Grease your air fryer with a non-stick cooking spray and add the chicken tenders.
5. Cook for 8 minutes at a 360 degrees Fahrenheit or until it turns golden brown.
6. Serve and enjoy!

Nutritional Information per serving:

Calories: 345, Fat: 11g, Protein: 32g, Carbohydrates: 9g, Dietary Fiber: 2.4g

Well-Tasted Popcorn Chicken

Time: 20 minutes

Yield: 2

Ingredients:

- 2 boneless, skinless chicken breasts
- 1 cup of breadcrumbs
- 2 beaten eggs
- 1 cup of flour
- 1 teaspoon of salt
- 1 teaspoon of black pepper
- 1 teaspoon of onion powder
- 1 teaspoon of garlic powder

Instructions:

1. Preheat your air fryer to 390 degrees Fahrenheit.
2. Using a food processor, add the chicken breasts and beat it until it minced properly.
3. Using two bowls, add the flour ,the eggs and mix it properly into the first bowl, then in the second bowl, add the breadcrumbs, seasonings and mix it properly.
4. Mold the minced chicken into small balls.
5. Cover the minced chicken in the flour, dip it into the egg wash, and then cover it with the seasoned breadcrumbs.
6. Place it inside your air fryer and cook it for 10 minutes at a 390 degrees Fahrenheit or until it is fully done.
7. Serve and enjoy!

Nutritional Information per serving:

Calories: 170, Fat: 17g, Protein: 14g, Dietary fiber: 0g, Carbohydrates: 13g

Easy Chicken Strips

Time: 20 minutes

Yield: 2

Ingredients:

- 2 boneless, skinless chicken breasts, sliced into strips
- ½ cup of shredded coconut
- ½ cup of oats
- 1 cup of panko breadcrumbs
- 1 cup of flour
- 2 beaten eggs
- 1 teaspoon of salt
- 1 teaspoon of black pepper
- 1 teaspoon of onion powder
- ½ teaspoon of garlic powder
- 1 teaspoon of smoked paprika

Instructions:

1. Preheat your air fryer to 360 degrees Fahrenheit.
2. Firstly, slice the chicken breasts into thin strips.
3. Using a bowl, add the oats, shredded coconut, breadcrumbs, seasonings and mix properly.
4. Pick a second bowl, add the egg and mix properly, then pick another bowl, add the flour and place it aside.
5. Dredge the strips in the flour, dip the strips into the egg wash, and cover it with the coconut breadcrumb mixture.
6. Grease your air fryer basket with a nonstick cooking spray.
7. Place the chicken breasts inside your air fryer and cook it for 8 minutes at a 360 degrees Fahrenheit.
8. Reduce the heat to 340 degrees Fahrenheit and cook it for an additional 5 minutes until it is done.
9. Serve and enjoy!

Nutritional Information per serving:

Calories: 130, Fat: 12g, Protein: 14g, Carbohydrates: 8g, Dietary Fiber: 0.9g

Savory Sriracha Chicken Drumsticks

Time: 1 hour

Yield: 6

Ingredients:

- 6 drumsticks
- 1 cup of sriracha
- ½ cup of honey
- ½ cup of melted butter
- 1 tablespoon of soy sauce
- 4 cloves of minced garlic
- 1 teaspoon of salt
- 1 teaspoon of black pepper

Instructions:

1. Preheat your air fryer to 390 degrees Fahrenheit.
2. Grease your air fryer basket with a nonstick cooking spray and add the chicken drumsticks.
3. Cook it inside your air fryer for 10 minutes at a 390 degrees Fahrenheit.
4. While still doing that, using a small bowl, add and mix the remaining ingredients.
5. After 10 minutes, remove the chicken drumsticks and brush it with the sriracha sauce.
6. Lower the heat to 360 degrees Fahrenheit and cook the drumsticks for an additional 10 minutes.
7. With the remaining sauce, microwave it inside your air fryer for 30 seconds or at most 1 minute.
8. Carefully remove the chicken drumsticks from your air fryer and cover it with the sriracha sauce again.
9. Serve and enjoy!

Nutritional Information per serving:

Calories: 290, Fat: 36g, Protein: 13g, Dietary Fiber: 0g, Carbohydrates: 22g

Chinese-Style Honey Garlic Chicken

Time: 35 minutes (plus 4 hours of marinating time)

Yield: 4

Ingredients:

- 1 pound of chicken wings
- 1 tablespoon of olive oil
- ¼ cup of soy sauce
- 3 cloves of minced garlic
- 1/3 cup of honey
- 1 teaspoon of white vinegar
- 1 teaspoon of garlic salt
- Green onions (for garnishing purpose)
- Sesame seeds (for garnishing purpose)

Instructions:

1. Using a bowl, add and mix the olive oil, soy sauce, garlic cloves, honey, white vinegar, and the garlic salt properly.
2. Add the chicken breasts and toss it until it gets properly covered.
3. Using a Ziploc bag, add the chicken wings, honey-garlic mixture and allow it to marinate for 4 hours or overnight.
4. Preheat your air fryer to 390 degrees Fahrenheit.
5. Using your baking accessory, add the chicken wings and honey-garlic mixture.
6. Place it inside your air fryer and cook it for 8 minutes at a 390 degrees Fahrenheit.
7. After 8 minutes, stir the chicken wings inside your baking accessory and cook it for an additional 10 minutes, then increase the temperature to 400 degrees Fahrenheit.
8. Garnish it with the green onions and the sesame seeds.
9. Serve and enjoy!

Nutritional Information per serving:

Calories: 200, Fat: 25g, Dietary Fiber: 0.1g, Carbohydrates: 8g, Protein: 27g

Rich Parmesan Crusted Chicken Breasts

Time: 30 minutes

Yield: 4

Ingredients:

- 4 small boneless, skinless chicken breasts
- 1 cup of panko bread crumbs
- ½ cup of Parmesan cheese
- 3 tablespoons of freshly chopped parsley
- 1 teaspoon of salt
- 1 teaspoon of black pepper
- 3 tablespoons of melted butter
- 3 tablespoons of fresh lime juice
- 2 garlic pressed cloves

Instructions:

1. Preheat your air fryer to 360 degrees Fahrenheit.
2. Using a bowl, add and mix the panko breadcrumbs, Parmesan cheese, parsley, salt, and the black pepper properly.
3. Pick another bowl, and mix the melted butter, fresh lime juice, and garlic.
4. Soak the chicken breasts into the butter mixture and cover it with the panko breadcrumb mixture until it is properly covered.
5. Grease your air fryer basket with a nonstick cooking spray and place the chicken breasts inside.
6. Cook it for 20 to 25 minutes inside your air fryer under a 360 degrees Fahrenheit of heat or until it turns golden brown and has a crispy texture.
7. Serve and enjoy!

Nutritional Information per serving:

Calories: 290, Fat: 16g, Protein: 59g, Dietary Fiber: 0.5g, Carbohydrates: 2.6g

Nashville Flaming Hot Breaded Chicken

Time: 35 minutes

Yield: 4

Ingredients:

- 4 medium or small chicken thighs
- 1 cup of buttermilk
- 2 beaten eggs
- ¼ cup of hot sauce

Flour Ingredients:

- 2 cups of flour
- 1 tablespoon of baking powder
- 1 tablespoon of cayenne pepper

Seasoning Spiced Rub Ingredients:

- 2 teaspoons of salt
- 2 teaspoons of paprika
- 2 teaspoons of onion powder
- 2 teaspoons of garlic powder
- 2 teaspoons of chili powder
- 2 teaspoons of black pepper
- 2 teaspoons of dried oregano
- 2 teaspoons of dried basil
- 1 tablespoon of cayenne pepper

Hot Sauce Ingredients:

- 2 tablespoons of hot sauce
- 2 tablespoons of melted butter
- 1 tablespoon of cayenne pepper
- 1 tablespoon of brown sugar
- 1 teaspoon of smoked paprika
- ¾ cup of olive oil

Instructions:

1. Using a small bowl, add and mix all the seasoning spiced rub ingredients properly.
2. Rub the chicken thighs with the seasoning mix and reserve any leftovers.
3. For the battered chicken: using a bowl, add and mix the buttermilk, eggs, and the ¼ cup of hot sauce properly.

4. Using another bowl, add 2 cups of flour, 1 tablespoon of baking powder, 1 tablespoon of cayenne pepper, any leftover spice rub and stir until it is properly mixed.
5. Dredge each chicken thigh into the flour, dip it into the buttermilk mixture and cover it with the flour once again.
6. Preheat your air fryer to 360 degrees Fahrenheit.
7. Place the chicken thighs into your air fryer and cook it for 8 minutes or until its done.
8. Thereafter, carefully remove it from your air fryer and allow it to cool off.
9. Using a small bowl, add and mix all the hot sauce ingredients, pour over the cooked chicken thighs and toss it until it is properly covered.
10. Serve and enjoy!

Nutritional Information per serving:

Calories: 380, Fat: 28g, Protein: 55g, Dietary Fiber: 3.5g, Carbohydrates: 19g

Desirable Korean Fried Chicken Wings

Time: 20 minutes

Yield: 4

Ingredients:

- 1 pound of chicken wings
- ½ cup of cornstarch
- 1 teaspoon of salt
- 1 teaspoon of black pepper
- 1 tablespoon of sesame seeds (for garnishing purposes)

Korean Dressing Ingredients:

- 4 tablespoons of Korean gojuchang
- 1 tablespoon of apple cider vinegar
- 1 tablespoon of melted butter
- 2 tablespoons of honey
- 1 tablespoon of soy sauce

Instructions:

1. Preheat your air fryer to 360 degrees Fahrenheit.
2. Using a bowl, season the chicken wings with the salt and black pepper.
3. Cover the chicken wings with the cornstarch.
4. Grease your air fryer basket with a nonstick cooking spray and add the chicken wings.
5. Cook it for 25 to 30 minutes or until it gets crispy, while still shaking it at a regular intervals of 8 minutes.
6. Using a bowl, add and mix all the Korean dressing ingredients properly.
7. Thereafter, carefully remove it from your air fryer and toss it with the Korean dressing mixture.
8. Garnish it with the sesame seeds.
9. Serve and enjoy!

Nutritional Information per serving:

Calories: 260, Fat: 16g, Protein: 15g, Dietary Fiber: 0.5g, Carbohydrates: 12g

Awesome Crispy Baked Garlic Parmesan Chicken Wings

Time: 40 minutes

Yield: 2

Ingredients:

- 1 pound of chicken wings
- 1 tablespoon of olive oil
- 2 tablespoons of melted butter
- 4 cloves of minced garlic
- 3 tablespoons of freshly chopped parsley
- 1 teaspoon of salt
- ½ cup of grated Parmesan cheese

Instructions:

1. Using a large pot, fill it with water and place a steamer basket into it.
2. Add the chicken wings on top of the steamer basket and allow it to steam for 12 minutes. Once it is done, remove it from the steamer basket and let it get cool off and dry.
3. Preheat your air fryer to 390 degrees Fahrenheit.
4. Grease your air fryer basket with a nonstick cooking spray and add the chicken wings.
5. Cook the chicken wings for 25 to 30 minutes or until it has a golden brown color and a crispy texture, while still shaking it at a regular intervals of 8minutes.
6. Using a saucepan, mix properly the olive oil, melted butter, garlic cloves, parsley, and the salt, while heating it on an average pressure of heat for 3 minutes. Thereafter remove and place it aside.
7. Remove the chicken wings from your air fryer and place it into a large bowl, pour the garlic mixture over the chicken wings and toss until it is properly covered.
8. Sprinkle the Parmesan cheese on it.
9. Serve and enjoy!

Nutritional Information per serving:

Calories: 510, Fat: 40g, Protein: 35g, Dietary Fiber: 0g, Carbohydrates: 3g

Spicy Teriyaki Chicken Wings

Time: 30 minutes (plus 4 hours of marinating time)

Yield: 4

Ingredients:

- 1 ½ pound of chicken wings
- ½ cup of soy sauce
- ¼ cup of rice wine vinegar
- ¼ cup of brown sugar
- 3 cloves of minced garlic
- 1 teaspoon of ginger powder
- 1 teaspoon of red pepper flakes
- 1 teaspoon of salt
- 1 teaspoon of black pepper

Instructions:

1. Using a bowl, add and mix the soy sauce, rice wine vinegar, brown sugar, garlic cloves, ginger powder, red pepper flakes, salt, and black pepper.
2. Then using a Ziploc bag, add the chicken wings, teriyaki mixture and allow it to marinate for 4 hours or overnight.
3. Preheat your air fryer to 390 degrees Fahrenheit.
4. Using your baking accessory, add the chicken wings and marinade it.
5. Place it inside your air fryer and cook it for 8 minutes at a pressure of 390 degrees Fahrenheit.
6. After 8 minutes, flip the chicken over and cook it for an additional 10 minutes, at this point increasing the temperature to 400 degrees Fahrenheit.
7. Serve and enjoy!

Nutritional Information per serving:

Calories: 220, Fat: 15g, Protein: 17g, Dietary Fiber: 0g, Carbohydrates: 3g

Chapter 8: Air Fryer Fish and Seafood

Remarkable Fish and Chips with Sauce

Time: 35 minutes

Yield: 4

Fish Ingredients:

- 4 cod fish fillets
- 1 teaspoon of olive oil
- 1 cup of flour
- 1 cup of panko breadcrumbs
- 2 beaten eggs

Fries Ingredients:

- 2 potatoes, cut into ½-inch strips
- 1 tablespoon of olive oil
- 1 teaspoon of salt

Sauce Ingredients:

- ¼ cup of mayonnaise
- 1 tablespoon of freshly chopped dill
- 1 tablespoon of freshly chopped tarragon
- 2 tablespoons of sour cream
- 2 tablespoons of finely chopped dill pickle
- 2 tablespoons of finely chopped red onion

Instructions:

1. Soak the potato pieces in a bowl of water for 30 minutes. After 30 minutes, drain it into a colander and pat it dry using a cloth.
2. Preheat your air fryer to 360 degrees Fahrenheit.
3. Using a large bowl, add and mix the potato strips, olive oil, salt and toss it until it is properly covered.
4. Place the potato strips inside your air fryer and cook it for 20 to 25 minutes, while still shaking it at a regular interval of 6 minutes until the potatoes reaches its golden brown color and crispy texture state. After that, remove and set it aside.
5. Then for the fish: Using a bowl, add the flour, pick another bowl, add the eggs and stir properly, then using another separate bowl, add the breadcrumbs and olive oil.
6. Dredge the cod fillets in the flour, dip it in the egg mixture, and then cover it with the breadcrumbs.

7. Grease your air fryer basket with a nonstick cooking spray and add the battered cod fillets.
8. Cook it for 10 minutes or until it has a golden brown color, carefully remove it from your air fryer basket and allow it to cool off.
9. For the sauce: Using a bowl, add all the mayonnaise, dill, tarragon, sour cream, dill pickle, the red onion, and stir it until it is properly mixed .
10. Serve and enjoy!

Nutritional Information per serving:

Calories: 250, Fat: 8g, Protein: 13g, Dietary Fiber: 2g, Carbohydrates: 3g

Grand Air-Fried Coconut Shrimp

Time:

Yield: 4

Ingredients:

- 1 pound of peeled and deveined shrimp
- 1 cup of shredded coconut
- 1 cup of panko breadcrumbs
- 2 eggs
- 1/3 cup of flour
- 1 teaspoon of salt
- 1 teaspoon of black pepper

Instructions:

1. Preheat your air fryer to 360 degrees Fahrenheit.
2. Using a bowl, add and mix the flour, salt, and black pepper. Then using a second bowl, add the eggs and beat it properly. Pick a third bowl, add and mix the shredded coconut and breadcrumbs.
3. Dredge each shrimp in the flour, dip it into the egg wash and then cover it with the coconut breadcrumb mixture.
4. Grease your air fryer basket with a nonstick cooking spray and add the shrimp.
5. Cook it for 10 to 15 minutes at a 360 degrees Fahrenheit or until it has a golden brown color.
6. Serve and enjoy!

'Nutritional Information per serving:

Calories: 250, Fat: 14g, Protein: 9g, Dietary Fiber: 1.6g, Carbohydrates: 4g

Splendid Salmon Patties

Time: 15 minutes

Yield: 2

Ingredients:

- 1 (14-ounce) can of drained canned salmon
- ¼ cup of chopped onion
- ¼ cup of ground oats
- ¼ cup of wheat flour
- 1 egg
- ¼ cup of mayonnaise
- 1 tablespoon of parsley
- 1 teaspoon of salt
- 1 teaspoon of black pepper
- 1 cup of breadcrumbs

Instructions:

1. Preheat your air fryer to 390 degrees Fahrenheit.
2. Using a bowl, add and mix the canned salmon, onion, ground oats, wheat flour, egg, parsley, salt, black pepper and the mayonnaise properly.
3. Divide the salmon mixture into 4 patties and cover it with the breadcrumbs.
4. Add the salmon patties inside your air fryer and cook it for 8 to 10 minutes or until it has a golden brown color.
5. Serve and enjoy!

Nutritional Information per serving:

Calories: 260, Fat: 15g, Protein: 16g, Dietary Fiber: 1g, Carbohydrates: 14g

Japanese-Style Fried Prawns

Time: 15 minutes

Yield: 2

Ingredients:

- 1 pound of peeled and deveined prawns
- 1 cup of rice flour
- 1 cup of panko bread crumbs
- 2 eggs
- 1 teaspoon of ground ginger
- 1 tablespoon of paprika
- 1 teaspoon of salt
- 1 teaspoon of black pepper
- 1 teaspoon of garlic powder

Instructions:

1. Preheat your air fryer to 380 degrees Fahrenheit.
2. Using a bowl, add the prawns, salt, black pepper, garlic powder, ground ginger and toss until it is properly mixed.
3. Then using another bowl, add the rice flour, paprika and mix it well. Pick a second bowl, add the eggs and beat it properly. Then using a third bowl, add the panko breadcrumbs.
4. Dredge the seasoned prawns into the flour, dip it into the egg wash, and then cover it with the panko breadcrumbs.
5. Grease your air fryer basket with a nonstick cooking spray and add the prawns.
6. Cook it for 8 minutes or until it has a golden brown color and repeat if necessary.
7. Serve and enjoy!

Nutritional Information per serving:

Calories: 210, Fat: 8g, Protein: 40g, Dietary Fiber: 0g, Carbohydrates: 4g

Great Air-Fried Soft-Shell Crab

Time:

Yield: 2

Ingredients:

- 2 soft-shell crabs
- 1 cup of flour
- 2 beaten eggs
- 1 cup of panko breadcrumbs
- 1 teaspoon of onion powder
- 1 teaspoon of garlic powder
- 1 teaspoon of salt
- 1 teaspoon of black pepper

Instructions:

1. Preheat your air fryer to 360 degrees Fahrenheit.
2. Using a bowl, add the flour, pick a second bowl, add the eggs and mix properly. Then using a third bowl, mix the panko breadcrumbs and the seasonings properly.
3. Grease your air fryer basket with a nonstick cooking spray and add the crabs inside.
4. Cook it inside your air fryer for 8 minutes or until it has a golden brown color.
5. Thereafter, carefully remove it from your air fryer and allow it to cool off.
6. Serve and enjoy!

Nutritional Information per serving:

Calories: 380, Fat: 16g, Protein: 24g, Carbohydrates: 9g, Dietary Fiber: 5g

Stunning Air-Fried Clams

Time: 15 minutes

Yield: 2

Ingredients:

- 1 (10-ounce) can of whole baby clams, drained and shucked
- 2 beaten eggs
- 1 cup of flour
- 1 cup of panko breadcrumbs
- 1 teaspoon of salt
- 1 teaspoon of black pepper
- 1 teaspoon of garlic powder
- 1 teaspoon of onion powder
- 1 teaspoon of cayenne pepper
- 1 tablespoon of dried oregano

Instructions:

1. Preheat your air fryer to 390 degrees Fahrenheit.
2. Using a bowl, add the flour, pick a second bowl, add the eggs and mix properly. Then using a third bowl, add and mix the panko breadcrumbs, seasonings, and the herbs properly.
3. Dredge the clams in the flour, immerse it into the egg wash and then cover it with the breadcrumb mixture.
4. Place the clams inside your air fryer and cook it for 2 minutes or until it has a golden brown color, while being cautious of overcooking.
5. Thereafter, carefully remove it from your air fryer and allow it to cool.
6. Serve and enjoy!

Nutritional Information per serving:

Calories: 225, Fat: 12g, Protein: 15g, Carbohydrates: 3g, Dietary Fiber: 0.5g

Mind-Blowing Air-Fried Crawfish with Cajun Dipping Sauce

Time: 10 minutes

Yield: 4

Ingredients:

- 1 pound of cooked craw-fish tail meat
- 1 beaten egg
- 4 chopped green onions
- 1 teaspoon of melted butter
- 1 teaspoon of salt
- 1 teaspoon of cayenne pepper
- 1 teaspoon of black pepper
- 1/3 cup of panko breadcrumbs
- 1/3 cup of bread flour

Sauce Ingredients:

- ¾ cup of mayonnaise
- ½ cup of ketchup
- 1 teaspoon of horseradish

Instructions:

1. Preheat your air fryer to 380 degrees Fahrenheit.
2. Using a bowl, add the eggs, green onion, butter, salt, cayenne pepper, black pepper and salt.
3. Add the panko breadcrumbs, bread flour and pour in the craw-fish, stirring it until it is properly covered.
4. Grease your air fryer basket with a nonstick cooking spray.
5. Add the battered craw-fish inside your air fryer and cook it for 5 minutes or until it has a golden brown color.
6. Thereafter, using a bowl, add the mayonnaise, ketchup, horseradish and mix properly.
7. Serve and enjoy!

Nutritional Information per serving:

Calories: 205, Fat: 16.7g, Protein: 26g, Dietary Fiber: 0.3g, Carbohydrates: 8.8g

Southern-Air-Fried Cat Fish

Time: 15 minutes

Yield: 4

Ingredients:

- 4 skinless catfish fillets
- 1 teaspoon of salt
- 1 teaspoon of black pepper
- 1 cup of cornmeal
- 1 cup of flour

Instructions:

1. Preheat your air fryer to 360 degrees Fahrenheit.
2. Using a bowl, add the cornmeal, flour, salt, black pepper and mix it properly.
3. Dredge the catfish fillets in the seasoned cornmeal mixture.
4. Grease your air fryer with a non-stick cooking spray and add the catfish fillets.
5. Cook the catfish for 8 minutes at a 360 degrees Fahrenheit or until it turns brown.
6. Serve and enjoy!

Nutritional Information per serving:

Calories: 350, Fat: 15g, Protein: 25g, Dietary Fiber: 0g, Carbohydrates: 36g

Wondrous Creole Fried Shrimp with Sriracha Sauce

Time: 10 minutes   Yield: 4

Ingredients:

- 1 pound of peeled and deveined shrimp
- ½ cup of cornmeal
- ½ cup of breadcrumbs
- 1 beaten egg
- 1 tablespoon of hot sauce
- 1 tablespoon of mustard
- 2 tablespoons of creole seasoning
- 1 teaspoon of onion powder
- 1 teaspoon of garlic powder
- 1 teaspoon of black pepper
- 1 teaspoon of salt

Siracha Sauce Ingredients:

- 1 cup of mayonnaise
- 3 tablespoons of sriracha sauce
- 1 tablespoon of soy sauce
- 1 teaspoon of black pepper

Instructions:

1. Preheat your air fryer to 360 degrees Fahrenheit.
2. Using a bowl, add the eggs, hot sauce, mustard, 1 tablespoon of creole seasoning, onion powder, garlic powder, black pepper, salt, the shrimp and toss until it is properly covered. Using another bowl, add the breadcrumbs, flour, 1 tablespoon of creole seasoning, the shrimp and cover it properly.
3. Grease your air fryer basket with a nonstick cooking spray and add the shrimp.
4. Cook for it for 5 minutes or until it has a golden brown color, while being careful not to overcook.
5. Thereafter, carefully remove it from your air fryer and allow it to cool.
6. Pick a separate bowl, add and mix all the sauce ingredients properly.Serve!

Nutritional Information per serving:

Calories: 200, Fat: 12g, Protein: 15g, Carbohydrates: 7g, Dietary Fiber: 0.6g

Chapter 9: Air Fryer Meat Recipes

Sweet and Spicy Montreal Steak

Time: 15 minutes

Yield: 2

Ingredients:

- 2 boneless sirloin steaks
- 1 tablespoon of olive oil
- 1 tablespoon of brown sugar
- 1 tablespoon of Montreal steak seasoning
- 1 teaspoon of crushed red pepper

Instructions:

1. Preheat your air fryer to 390 degrees Fahrenheit.
2. Sprinkle the sirloin steaks with olive oil.
3. Rub each steak with the brown sugar, Montreal steak seasoning, and the crushed red pepper.
4. Place the baking accessory inside your air fryer and add it to the steaks inside.
5. Cook it for 3 minutes at a 390 degrees Fahrenheit.
6. After 3 minutes has elapsed, flip the steak over and cook it for an additional 3 minutes or until it reaches your desired texture.
7. Carefully remove it from your air fryer and allow it to cool before slicing them into strips.
8. Serve and enjoy!

Nutritional Information per serving:

Calories: 160, Fat: 5g, Protein: 25g, Dietary Fiber: 0g, Carbohydrates: 3g

Stunning Chicken Sandwich

Time: 25 minutes

Yield: 2

Ingredients:

- 2 boneless, skinless chicken breasts
- 1 cup of flour
- 2 beaten eggs
- 1 teaspoon of garlic powder
- 1 teaspoon of onion powder
- 1 teaspoon of salt
- 1 teaspoon of black pepper
- 4 toasted hamburger buns

Instructions:

1. Using a bowl, add and mix the flour and seasonings properly. Then in a second bowl, add the eggs and beat it well.
2. Dip the chicken breasts into the egg mixture and remove any excess batter.
3. Dredge the chicken breasts in the flour mixture until it is properly coated.
4. Preheat your air fryer to 340 degrees Fahrenheit.
5. Grease your air fryer basket with a nonstick cooking spray.
6. Add the chicken breasts and cook for 6 minutes at a 340 degrees Fahrenheit.
7. Flip the chicken breasts and cook it for an additional 6 minutes.
8. Then increase the temperature to 400 degrees Fahrenheit and cook it for 2 minutes per side.
9. Serve and enjoy on the toasted hamburger buns, or with any toppings you desire!

Nutritional Information per serving:

Calories: 265, Fat:1 7g, Protein: 21g, Dietary Fiber: 1.2g, Carbohydrates: 5g

Hearty Hot Dogs

Time: 10 minutes

Yield: 2

Ingredients:

- 2 hot dogs
- 2 hot dog buns
- Any hot dog toppings if desired

Instructions:

1. Preheat your air fryer to 390 degrees Fahrenheit.
2. Put the hot dogs inside your air fryer and cook it for 5 minutes.
3. Carefully remove it from your air fryer and allow it to cool off.
4. Place the cooked hot dogs in the bun and add any desired toppings.
5. Serve and enjoy!

Nutritional Information per serving:

Calories: 110, Fat: 10g, Protein: 5g, Dietary Fiber: 0g, Carbohydrates: 2g

Sweet and Sour Pork

Time: 30 minutes

Yield: 4

Ingredients:

- 2 pounds of chopped into 1-inch pieces boneless pork
- 2 beaten eggs
- 1 cup of cornstarch
- 3 tablespoons of oil
- 1 teaspoon of salt
- 1 teaspoon of black pepper

Sweet and Sour Sauce Ingredients:

- ½ cup of sugar
- 5 tablespoons of ketchup
- ½ cup of seasoned rice vinegar
- 1 tablespoon of soy sauce
- ½ teaspoon of salt

Instructions:

1. Preheat your air fryer to 340 degrees Fahrenheit.
2. Using a bowl, add the eggs and beat it properly. Pick another bowl, add and mix the cornstarch, salt, black pepper and properly and set it aside.
3. Dredge each pork chunks into the cornstarch mixture, dip it in the egg wash, and then cover it with the cornstarch mixture.
4. Grease your air fryer basket with a nonstick cooking spray.
5. Place the pork chunks in your air fryer basket and cook it for 8 to 12 minutes at a 340 degrees Fahrenheit, shaking it halfway through.
6. Then, using a saucepan, add all the sweet and sour sauce ingredients and heat it under an average pressure of heat for around 5 minutes, while still stirring consistently.
7. Once the pork turns golden brown and crispy, carefully remove it from your air fryer and allow it to cool off. Serve and enjoy with the sauce!

Nutritional Information per serving:

Calories: 360, Fat: 19g, Protein: 14g, Dietary Fiber: 0g, Carbohydrates: 6g

Yummy Rodeo Sirloin Steaks with Coffee Rub

Time: 25 minutes

Yield: 2

Ingredients:

- 2 boneless sirloin steaks
- 1 tablespoon of olive oil
- 2 tablespoons of ground coffee
- 1 tablespoon of salt
- 1 tablespoon of brown sugar
- 1 tablespoon of dried thyme
- 1 teaspoon of garlic powder
- 1 teaspoon of black pepper

Instructions:

1. Preheat your air fryer to 390 degrees Fahrenheit.
2. Sprinkle the sirloin steak with the olive oil.
3. Using a bowl, add the ground coffee, salt, brown sugar, dried thyme, garlic powder, black pepper and mix properly.
4. Rub each sirloin steak with the coffee rub until it is properly covered.
5. Place the baking accessory inside your air fryer and add it to the steak inside.
6. Cook it for 3 minutes at a 390 degrees Fahrenheit.
7. After 3 minutes, flip the steak over and cook for an additional 3 minutes or until it reaches your desired texture.
8. Carefully remove it from your air fryer and allow it to cool before slicing.
9. Serve and enjoy!

Nutritional Information per serving:

Calories: 480, Fat: 29g, Protein: 45g, Carbohydrates: 8g, Dietary Fiber: 0.2g

Chapter 10: Air Fryer Vegetable and Sides Recipes

Supreme Air-Fried Tofu

Time: 55 minutes

Yield: 4

Ingredients:

- 1 block of pressed and sliced into 1-inch cubes of extra-firm tofu
- 2 tablespoons of soy sauce
- 1 teaspoon of seasoned rice vinegar
- 2 teaspoons of toasted sesame oil
- 1 tablespoon of cornstarch

Instructions:

1. Using a bowl, add and toss the tofu, soy sauce, seasoned rice vinegar, sesame oil until it is properly covered.
2. Place it inside your refrigerator and allow to marinate for 30 minutes.
3. Preheat your air fryer to 370 degrees Fahrenheit.
4. Add the cornstarch to the tofu mixture and toss it until it is properly covered.
5. Grease your air fryer basket with a nonstick cooking spray and add the tofu inside your basket.
6. Cook it for 20 minutes at a 370 degrees Fahrenheit, and shake it after 10 minutes.
7. Serve and enjoy!

Nutritional Information per serving:

Calories: 80, Fat: 5.8g, Protein: 5g, Carbohydrates: 3g, Dietary Fiber: 1.2g

Not Your Average Zucchini Parmesan Chips

Time: 15 minutes

Yield: 4

Ingredients:

- 2 thinly sliced zucchinis
- 1 beaten egg
- ½ cup of panko breadcrumbs
- ½ cup of grated Parmesan cheese
- 1 teaspoon of salt
- 1 teaspoon of black pepper

Instructions:

1. Prepare your zucchini by using a mandolin or a knife to slice the zucchinis thinly.
2. Use a cloth to pat dry the zucchini chips.
3. Then using a bowl, add the eggs and beat it properly. After that, pick another bowl, and add the breadcrumbs, Parmesan cheese, salt, and black pepper.
4. Dredge the zucchini chips into the egg mixture and then cover it with the Parmesan-breadcrumb mixture.
5. Grease the battered zucchini chips with a nonstick cooking spray and place it inside your air fryer.
6. Cook it for 8 minutes at a 350 degrees Fahrenheit.
7. Once done, carefully remove it from your air fryer and sprinkle another teaspoon of salt to give it some taste.
8. Serve and enjoy!

Nutritional Information per serving:

Calories: 100, Fat: 16g, Protein: 4g, Carbohydrates 9g, Dietary Fiber: 1.8g

Outstanding Batter-Fried Scallions

Time: 10 minutes

Yield: 4

Ingredients:

- 4 bunches of trimmed scallions
- 1 cup of flour
- 1 cup of white wine
- 1 teaspoon of salt
- 1 teaspoon of black pepper

Instructions:

1. Preheat your air fryer to 390 degrees Fahrenheit.
2. Using a bowl, add and mix the white wine, the flour and stir until it gets smooth.
3. Add the salt, the black pepper and mix again.
4. Dip each scallion into the flour mixture until it is properly covered and remove any excess batter.
5. Grease your air fryer basket with a nonstick cooking spray and add the scallions. At this point, you may need to work in batches.
6. Cook the scallions for 3 to 5 minutes or until it has a golden brown color and crispy texture, while still shaking it after every 2 minutes.
7. Carefully remove it from your air fryer and check if it's properly done. Then allow it to cool before serving.
8. Serve and enjoy!

Nutritional Information per serving:

Calories: 190, Fat: 22g, Protein: 4g, Carbohydrates: 9g, Dietary Fiber: 0.8g

Delectable French Green Beans with Shallots and Almonds

Time: 25 minutes

Yield: 4

Ingredients:

- 1 ½ pounds of stemmed French green beans
- ½ pound of peeled, stemmed quartered shallots
- ¼ cup of lightly toasted silvered almonds
- 2 tablespoons of olive oil
- 1 tablespoon of salt
- 1 teaspoon of garlic salt
- 1 teaspoon of white pepper

Instructions:

1. Using a large pot, fill it with water and boil it under an average pressure of heat.
2. Add the green beans, a tablespoon of salt, stir for a while and cook it for 2 minutes.
3. Once done, drain it using a colander and allow it to cool off.
4. Using a large bowl, add the green beans, shallots, garlic salt, white pepper, olive oil and toss it until it is properly covered.
5. Place the green beans and shallots inside your air fryer basket and cook it for 25 minutes at a 400 degrees Fahrenheit, shaking it halfway through.
6. Then pick a large bowl, add the cooked green beans, shallots, almonds and toss it until it is properly covered.
7. Serve and enjoy!

Nutritional Information per serving:

Calories: 110, Fat: 9g, Protein: 3g, Carbohydrates: 7g, Dietary Fiber: 4g

Super-Healthy Air-Fried Green Tomatoes

Time: 25 minutes

Yield: 4

Ingredients:

- 4 sliced into ¼-inch pieces green tomatoes
- 2 beaten eggs
- 2 tablespoons of milk
- 1 cup of flour
- ½ cup of cornmeal
- ½ cup of panko breadcrumbs
- 1 teaspoon of garlic powder
- 1 teaspoon of paprika
- 1 teaspoon of salt
- 1 teaspoon of black pepper

Instructions:

1. Using a bowl, add 1 cup of flour.
2. Pick a second bowl, add the eggs, milk and mix properly.
3. Using a third bowl, add the cornmeal, panko breadcrumbs, seasonings and mix properly.
4. For each tomato slice, dredge it in the flour, dip it into the egg mixture and then cover it with the cornmeal-breadcrumb mixture.
5. Grease your air fryer basket with a nonstick cooking spray.
6. Working in batches, add the green tomatoes, cook it for 20 minutes at a 360 degrees Fahrenheit of heat, and flip it after 10 minutes.
7. Repeat the above step with any leftover.
8. Serve and enjoy!

Nutritional Information per serving:

Calories: 190, Fat: 12g, Protein: 4g, Dietary Fiber: 6g, Protein: 4.25g

Luscious Air-Fried Broccoli Crisps

Time: 35 minutes

Yield: 4

Ingredients:

- 1 large chopped into florets broccoli head
- 2 tablespoons of olive oil
- 1 teaspoon of salt
- 1 teaspoon of black pepper

Instructions:

1. Preheat your air fryer to 360 degrees Fahrenheit.
2. Using a bowl, add and toss the broccoli florets with the olive oil, salt, and black pepper.
3. Add the broccoli florets and cook it for 12 minutes, then shake after 6 minutes.
4. Carefully remove it from your air fryer and allow it to cool off.
5. Serve and enjoy!

Nutritional Information per serving:

Calories: 120, Fat: 19g, Protein: 4.5g, Carbohydrates: 8.3g, Dietary Fiber: 4.5g

Chapter 11: Air Fryer Desert Recipes

Toothsome Caramel Cheesecake

Time: 1 hour

Yield: 8

Crust Ingredients

- 2 cups of graham cracker crumbs
- ¼ cup of brown sugar
- ½ cup of melted butter

Filling Ingredients:

- 3 (8-ounce) package of softened cream cheese
- 1 cup of brown sugar
- 3 eggs
- ¾ cup of whipping cream
- ¼ cup of coffee syrup

Caramel Sauce Ingredients:

- ½ cup of butter
- 1 ¼ cup of brown sugar
- 2 tablespoons of coffee syrup
- ½ cup of whipping cream
- 1 teaspoon of salt

Instructions:

1. Preheat your air fryer to 360 degrees Fahrenheit.
2. Apply the flour to the sides and bottoms of a spring form pan.
3. Using a bowl, add and mix all the crust ingredients properly.
4. Press the crust down into the spring form pan.
5. Then using a large mixing bowl, add and beat all the filling ingredients properly.
6. Pour the filling over the crust.
7. Place it inside your air fryer and cook it for 15 minutes.
8. Reduce the heat to 320 degrees Fahrenheit and cook it for 10 more minutes.
9. Finally, reduce the heat to 300 degrees Fahrenheit and cook it for 15 minutes.
10. Then, carefully remove it from the oven and refrigerate it for 6 hours or overnight.
11. Thereafter, using a saucepan, melt the butter under an average pressure of heat.
12. Add the brown sugar, salt, coffee syrup and mix them properly.

13. Boil and cook it for 1 minute, while still stirring consistently until the brown sugar liquefies.
14. Pour in the whipping cream, turn off the heat and thereafter allow it to cool off for 10 minutes.
15. Spread the caramel sauce over the cheesecake.
16. Serve and enjoy!

Nutritional Information per serving:

Calories: 420, Fat: 25g, Protein: 5g, Dietary Fiber: 0g, Carbohydrates: 10g

Conclusion

Hopefully, after going through this book and trying out a couple of recipes, you will get to understand the flexibility and utility of the air fryers. It is certainly a multipurpose kitchen appliance that is highly recommended to everybody as it presents one with a palatable atmosphere to enjoy fried foods that are not only delicious but healthy, cheaper, and more convenient. The use of this kitchen appliance ensures that the making of some of your favorite snacks and meals will be carried out in a stress free manner without hassling around, which invariably legitimizes its worth and gives you a value for your money.

This book will be your all-time guide to understanding the basics of the air fryer and Atkins Diet, because with all the recipes mentioned in the book, it is rest assured that it will be something that you and the rest of the people around the world will enjoy for the rest of your lives. Also after going through this book , you will be able to prepare delicious and flavorsome meals that will not only be easy to carry out, but tasty and healthy as well.

However, you should never limit yourself to the recipes solely mentioned in this cookbook, go on and try new things! Explore new recipes! Experiment with different ingredients, seasonings and different methods! Create some new recipes and keep your mind open. By so doing you will be able to get the best out of your air fryer.

In a nutshell, if you found this book helpful, please kindly take the time to leave an honest review on Amazon. Your feedback will be greatly appreciated. Thank you, and the best wishes to you!

CPSIA information can be obtained
at www.ICGtesting.com
Printed in the USA
LVHW101609260120
644831LV00008B/296